THIRD

WORLDLINK

Developing English Fluency

Level 2

James R. Morgan

Nancy Douglas

NATIONAL GEOGRAPHIC LEARNING | CENGAGE Learning

Australia • Brazil • Mexico • Singapore • United Kingdom • United States

World Link Level 2: Developing English Fluency, Third Edition
James R. Morgan, Author
Nancy Douglas, Author
Susan Stempleski, Series Editor

Publisher: Sherrise Roehr

Executive Editor: Sarah Kenney

Senior Development Editor: Brenden Layte

Associate Development Editor: Alison Bruno

Assistant Editor: Patricia Giunta

Media Researcher: Leila Hishmeh

Senior Technology Product Manager:
 Lauren Krolick

Director of Global Marketing: Ian Martin

Senior Product Marketing Manager:
 Caitlin Thomas

Sr. Director, ELT & World Languages:
 Michael Burggren

Production Manager: Daisy Sosa

Content Project Manager: Beth Houston

Senior Print Buyer: Mary Beth Hennebury

Composition: Lumina

Cover/Text Design: Brenda Carmichael

Art Director: Brenda Carmichael

Cover Image: Sebastio Moreira/EPA/Alamy
Stock Photo

Inside Front Cover Image: AFP/Getty Images

Photo Credits are listed on the inside back cover.

For product information and technology assistance, contact us at
Cengage Learning Customer & Sales Support, 1-800-354-9706
For permission to use material from this text or product,
submit all requests online at **www.cengage.com/permissions**
Further permissions questions can be emailed to
permissionrequest@cengage.com

World Link 2 ISBN: 978-1-305-65099-2

World Link 2 + My World Link Online ISBN: 978-1-305-65100-5

National Geographic Learning
20 Channel Center Street
Boston, MA 02210
USA

Cengage Learning is a leading provider of customized learning solutions with employees residing in nearly 40 different countries and sales in more than 125 countries around the world. Find your local representative at **www.cengage.com**

Cengage Learning products are represented in Canada by Nelson Education, Ltd.

Visit National Geographic Learning online at ngl.cengage.com
Visit our corporate website at **cengage.com**

Printed in the United States of America
Print Number: 05   Print Year: 2017

Acknowledgments

We would like to extend a very special thank you to the Instituto Cultural Peruano Norteamericano (ICPNA) academic management staff in the central office, branches and teachers, for the helpful insights and suggestions that contributed toward the development of this series.

We would also like to thank Raúl Billini, Educational Consultant, Santo Domingo, Dominican Republic, for his contributions to this series.

Thank you to the educators who provided invaluable feedback throughout the development of the *World Link* series: Rocio Abarca, Instituto Tecnológico de Costa Rica / FUNDATEC; David Aduviri, CBA (Centro Boliviano Americano) - La Paz; Ramon Aguilar, Universidad Tecnológica de Hermosillo; Miguel Arrazola, CBA (Centro Boliviano Americano) - Santa Cruz; Cecilia Avila, Universidad de Xalapa; Isabel Baracat, CCI (Centro de Comunicação Inglesa); Daniel Sanchez Bedoy, Calfornia Language Center; Andrea Brotto, CEICOM (Centro de Idiomas para Comunidades); George Bozanich, Soongsil University; Emma Campo, Universidad Central; Andrea Carlson, Aichi Prefectural University; Martha Carrasco, Universidad Autonoma de Sinaloa; Herbert Chavel, Korea Advanced Institute of Science and Technology; J. Ventura Chavez, Universidad de Guadalajara CUSUR; Denise de Bartolomeo, AMICANA (Asociación Mendocina de Intercambio Cultural Argentino Norteamericano); Rodrigo de Campos Rezende, SEVEN Idiomas; John Dennis, Hokuriku University; Kirvin Andrew Dyer, Yan Ping High School; Marilena Fernandes, Alumni; Mark Firth, J.F. Oberlin University; Daniela Frillochi, ARICANA (Asociación Rosarina de Intercambio Cultural Argentino Norteamericano); Joseph Gabriella, Toyo University; Marina Gonzalez, Instituto Universitario de Lenguas Modernas; Robert Gordon, Korea Advanced Institute of Science and Technology; Scott Grigas, Youngsan University Gu Yingruo, Research Institute of Xiangzhou District, ZhuHai; Kyle Hammel, Incheon National University; Mariana Gil Hammer, Instituto Cultural Dominico Americano; Helen Hanae, Toyo University; Xu Heng, Nantong Polytechnic College; Amiris Helena, Centro Cultural Dominico Americano; Rafael Hernandez, Centro Educacional Tlaquepaque; Yo-Tien Ho, Takming University; Marie Igwe, Hanseo University; Roxana Jimenez, Instituto Tecnológico de Costa Rica / FUNDATEC; Liu Jing, Shanghai Foreign Language Education Press; Lâm Nguyễn Huỳnh, Van Lang University; Hui-Chuan Liao, National Kaohsiung University of Applied Sciences; Pan Lang, Nanjing Sport Institute; Sirina Kainongsuang, Perfect Publishing Company Limited; Karen Ko, ChinYi University; Ching-Hua Lin, National Taiwan University of Science and Technology; Simon Liu, ChinYi University; Maria Helena Luna, Tronwell; Ady Marrero, Alianza Cultural Uruguay Estados Unidos; Nancy Mcaleer, ELC Universidad Interamericana de Panama; Michael McCallister, Feng Chia University Language Center; José Antonio Mendes Lopes, ICBEU (Instituto Cultural Brasil Estados Unidos); Tania Molina, Instituto Tecnológico de Costa Rica / FUNDATEC; Iliana Mora, Instituto Tecnológico de Costa Rica / FUNDATEC; Fernando Morales, Universidad Tecnológica de Hermosillo; Vivian Morghen, ICANA (Instituto Cultural Argentino Norteamericano); Aree Na Nan, Chiang Mai University; He Ning, Nanjing Mochou Vocational School; Paul Nugent, Kkottongnae University; Niu Yuchun, New Oriental School Beijing; Elizabeth Ortiz, COPEI (Copol English Institute); Virginia Ortiz, Universidad Autonoma de Tamaulipas; Marshall Presnick, Language Link Vietnam; Justin Prock, Pyeongtaek University; Peter Reilly, Universidad Bonaterra; Ren Huijun, New Oriental School Hangzhou; Andreina Romero, URBE (Universidad Rafael Belloso Chacín); Leon Rose, Jeonju University; Chris Ruddenklau, Kinki University; Adelina Ruiz, Instituto Tecnologico de Estudios Superiores de Occidente; Eleonora Salas, IICANA (Instituto de Intercambio Cultural Argentino Norteamericano); Jose Salas, Universidad Tecnológica del Norte de Guanajuato; Mary Sarawit, Naresuan University International College; Jenay Seymour, Hong-ik University; Huang Shuang, Shanghai International Studies University; Sávio Siqueira, ACBEU (Asociação Cultural Brasil Estados Unidos) / UFBA (Universidade Federal da Bahia); Beatriz Solina, ARICANA (Asociación Rosarina de Intercambio Cultural Argentino Norteamericano); Mari Cruz Suárez, Servicio de Idiomas UAM; Bambang Sujianto, Intensive English Course (IEC); Howard Tarnoff, Health Sciences University of Hokkaido; Emily J Thomas, Incheon National University; Sandrine Ting, St. John's University; Tran Nguyen Hoai Chi, Vietnam USA Society English Training Service Center; Ruth Tun, Universidad Autonoma de Campeche; Rubén Uceta, Centro Cultural Dominico Americano; Maria Inés Valsecchi, Universidad Nacional de Río Cuarto; Alicia Vazquez, Instituto Internacional; Patricia Veciño, ICANA (Instituto Cultural Argentino Norteamericano); Punchalee Wasanasomsithi, Chulalongkorn University; Tomoe Watanabe, Hiroshima City University; Dhunyawat Treenate, Rajamangala University of Technology Krungthep; Haibo Wei, Nantong Agricultural College; Tomohiro Yanagi, Chubu University; Jia Yuan, Global IELTS School; Selestin Zainuddin, LBPP-LIA.

Unit / Lesson	Video	Vocabulary	Listening

Grammar	Pronunciation	Speaking	Reading	Writing	Communication
The simple present tense vs. the present continuous tense pp. 8, 193 Review of the simple past tense pp. 14, 194	Question stress p. 6	Introducing a person to someone else / Responding to introductions p. 7	Try, try again! p. 12 Understand the main idea Read for details Summarize Synthesize information	Write about something you learned p. 15	Guessing classmates' identities based on their habits p. 9 Talking about high school p. 15
The comparative form of adjectives pp. 22, 195 The superlative form of adjectives pp. 28, 196	Sentence stress and rhythm p. 20	Making suggestions / Responding to suggestions p. 21	The healthiest lifestyle in the world? p. 26 Skim for the main idea Make predictions Check predictions Scan for information	Write a restaurant review p. 29	Describing changes to a restaurant p. 23 Creating a menu for a new restaurant and making plans to go out to eat p. 29
Stative verbs pp. 36, 197 Modals of present possibility pp. 42, 198	Dropped syllables p. 34	Talking about possibility p. 35	Mysterious artwork p. 40 Make predictions Scan for details Identify main ideas Read for details	Do research and write about an issue p. 42	Talking about intuition p. 37 Describing an explanation to a mystery p. 43
Quantity expressions pp. 54, 199 Giving advice with *could*, *should*, *ought to*, and *had better* pp. 60, 200	Unstressed *of* p. 54	Disagreeing / Disagreeing more strongly p. 53	Trendspotting p. 58 Make predictions Check predictions Read for gist Sentence insertion Understand paraphrases	Give fashion advice to someone looking for a job p. 60	Making decisions and stating opinions p. 55 Taking a fashion quiz and giving adice p. 61
Requests with modal verbs and *mind* pp. 68, 201 Modifiers *really* / *very* and *pretty* pp. 74, 202	Reduced forms of *could you* and *would you* p. 66	Making appointments p. 67	I love my neighborhood p. 72 Skim for the main idea Read for details Scan for information	Write about your neighborhood p. 74	Planning and describing a cleaning service p. 69 Describing improvements for your community p. 75
Plans and decisions with *be going to* and *will* pp. 82, 203 Predictions with *be going to* and *will* pp. 88, 204	Reduced form of *going to* p. 82	Responding to bad news / Offering to help p. 81	A different road to success p. 86 Draw conclusions Infer meaning Scan for details Identify pros and cons	Write about your college experience p. 89	Asking and answering questions about future plans p. 83 Making predictions about someone's future p. 89

SCOPE & SEQUENCE

Grammar	Pronunciation	Speaking	Reading	Writing	Communication
Agreeing with other people's statements: *so, too, neither,* and *either* pp. 100, 205 Time clauses with *before, after, when* pp. 106, 206	Reduced *want to* p. 99	Inviting someone to do something / Accepting or refusing an invitation p. 99	Get ready to get dirty p. 104 Make predictions Draw conclusions Read for details Scan for details Categorize information	Write about a holiday or festival in your country p. 107	Planning a party p. 101 Planning and describing an unusual holiday p. 107
The past continuous tense: statements / questions pp. 114, 207 Adverbs of manner pp. 120, 209	Compound words p. 113	Keeping a story going p. 113	The Cinderella story p. 118 Use background knowledge Identify main ideas Scan for details	Write an email about a previous event p. 121	Telling an unusual story p. 115 Describe a scene from a picture p. 121
The present perfect tense pp. 128, 210 Verb + infinitive pp. 134, 211	Reduced *for* in time expressions p. 128	Interviewing for a job p. 127	Asher Jay: creative conservationist p. 132 Make predictions Identify main ideas Scan for details Infer information	Write a presentation about an interesting career p. 134	Responding to job ads p. 129 Giving a presentation and providing feedback p. 135
Asking for permission pp. 146, 212 Verb + infinitive vs. verb + gerund pp. 152, 213	Stress in clarification questions p. 144	Using the telephone p. 145	Phone-free on the road? p. 150 Read for the gist Read for opinions Infer meaning Summarize and evaluate Exemplify	Describe your phone use p. 153	Giving and taking messages on the phone p. 147 Stating and supporting your opinion p. 153
Used to pp. 160, 214 Comparisons with *as... as* pp. 166, 215	*Used to* p. 160	Offering a counterargument p. 159	Robots to the rescue p. 164 Make predictions Infer meaning Sequence events	Compare products p. 167	Describing life changes p. 161 Designing and describing your own robot p. 167
Modal verbs of necessity pp. 174, 217 Present perfect (indefinite time) vs. simple past pp. 180, 217	Reduced *have to* and *has to* p. 172	Saying you've forgotten something p. 173	Going solo is the way to go! p. 178 Make predictions Guess meaning from context Read for details Scan for details	Correspond with a homeshare host p. 180	Deciding what to take on a trip p. 175 Making plans with a homeshare host p. 181

Language Summaries p. 186   **Grammar Notes** p. 193

1 MY LIFE

A college student in Baghdad, Iraq rides a motorcycle with his friends.

Look at the photo. Answer the questions.

1 What is the man doing?

2 How do you think the men in the photo know each other?

3 Does this activity look fun to you? Why or why not?

UNIT GOALS

1 Talk about the important people in your life

2 Introduce a person to someone else

3 Talk about classes and lessons you're taking

4 Describe something you learned to do

LESSON A PEOPLE

Shabana Basij-Rasikh talks with students at her school.

1 VIDEO Inside Afghanistan's First Boarding School for Girls

A Read the sentences and answer the questions.

Shabana Basij-Rasikh is an educator at SOLA (the School of Leadership, Afghanistan). It is the first girl's boarding school in Afghanistan.

1. What is a boarding school? (Use your dictionary to find out.)
2. Would you like to go to a boarding school? Why or why not?

> **Word Bank**
>
> *educator* = a teacher
>
> *leader* = a person who inspires and manages other people

B ▶ Read the sentences before you watch. Then watch the video about SOLA. Complete the sentences with the missing words.

1. When Shabana Basij-Rasikh was young, there were no ___SCHOOLS___ for ___GIRLS___.
2. ___6 %___ percent of women in Afghanistan have a college degree.
3. Shabana needed to become an ___EDUCATOR___.
4. She is the ___PRESIDENT___ and cofounder of SOLA.
5. At SOLA, they create a ___SAFE___ space for girls.
6. The girls come to SOLA to learn to become future ___LEADERS___.
7. When you educate a girl, you educate her ___FAMILY___, _HER COMMUNITY,_ _HER SOCIETY_ and the world.

> SIBLINGS
> PRIORITY
> PRIVILEGED
> SERVE
> EMPOWER

C 👥 Get into small groups and check your answers from **B**. What do you think of SOLA? Discuss.

2 VOCABULARY

A Read about the people in Mario's life. Complete the sentences with a word for each person.

> acquaintance   classmate   coworker / colleague
> friend   girlfriend / boyfriend   neighbor

Jason is Mario's _____ FRIEND _____.

We're best friends. We met when we were in elementary school.

Lei is Mario's _____ GIRLFRIEND _____.

We both attended the same school last year. We met and started going out.

Hakim is a(n) _____ AN ACQUAINTANCE _____ of Mario's.

We met once at a party, but I don't know him well. He seems like a nice guy.

Emma is Mario's _____ CLASSMATE _____.

We go to the same college and have two classes together this year.

Julia is a(n) _____ A COWORKER _____ of Mario's.

We work together in the same office, but in different departments.

David is Mario's _____ NEIGHBOR _____.

We live on the same street.

My name is **Mario**. I'm a student at City College. I also work part time in an office.

B Look at the words in blue and think of people in your life. On a piece of paper, write *People I Know* at the top of the page. List five people and write a sentence or two about each one.

C Tell your partner about the people in your life.

> Sergio is my friend. We met in class last year.

3 LISTENING

A 🔊 **Pronunciation: Question stress.** Listen and repeat. **CD 1 Track 2**

1. A: Is he your <u>boyfriend</u>?
   B: No, we're just friends.

2. A: Is he <u>your</u> boyfriend?
   B: No, he's going out with Maria.

3. A: Is <u>he</u> your boyfriend?
   B: No, <u>he</u> is.

B 🔊 **Pronunciation: Question stress.** Say these three sentences and responses.
Then listen for the stressed word in each sentence. Choose the best answer (a or b). **CD 1 Track 3**

1. Are you a <u>student</u> at City College?
   (a.) No, I work there.
   b. No, I go to Essex College.

2. I thought you were her <u>classmate.</u>
   a. No, my brother is.
   (b.) No, we go to different schools.

3. I think his best friend lives <u>next door</u>, right?
   a. No, I think it's his colleague.
   (b.) No, I think he lives down the street.

C 🔊 **Listen for gist.** Listen to the conversations and number the pictures in the order (1, 2, 3) you hear them. **CD 1 Track 4**

D 🔊 **Listen for details.** Read the sentences about each conversation. Then listen again and circle the correct answers. **CD 1 Track 4**

1. a. They are / aren't dating now.
   b. They are / aren't friends now.

2. a. They are / aren't friends.
   b. They know / don't know each other well.

3. a. They know / don't know each other.
   b. They are / aren't classmates now.

E 👥 **Exemplify.** Look at your answers in **D**. Choose one of the situations and create a short dialog with a partner. Perform it for another pair.

4 SPEAKING

A 🔊 Listen to the conversations. Which one is more informal? In each conversation, who is meeting for the first time? **CD 1 Track 5**

Conversation 1

MARIA: Hi, Junko.

JUNKO: Hi, Maria. It's good to see you again! How are you?

MARIA: Fine. How about you?

JUNKO: Pretty good.

MARIA: Oh, and this is my friend Ricardo. We both go to City University.

JUNKO: Hey, Ricardo. Nice to meet you.

RICARDO: Yeah, you too.

Conversation 2

MR. OTANI: Morning, Miriam.

MIRIAM: Good morning, Mr. Otani. Oh, Mr. Otani, I'd like you to meet Andres Garcia. He started working here yesterday. Andres, Mr. Otani is our V.P. of Sales.

MR. OTANI: Nice to meet you, Andres.

ANDRES: It's very nice to meet you, too, Mr. Otani.

B 👥 What does Maria say to introduce Ricardo? What does Miriam say to introduce Andres? Underline your answers. Then practice the conversations in a group of three.

SPEAKING STRATEGY

C 👥 Work in groups of three. Follow the steps below.

1. **Student A:** Choose a famous person to be. Write down your identity on a piece of paper and give it to Student B.

2. **Student B:** Read the identity of Student A. Then introduce Student A to Student C formally. Use the Useful Expressions to help you.

3. **Student C:** Respond to the introduction.

4. Change roles and follow steps 1 and 2 again.

D 👥 Now introduce the "famous friends" you met in **C** to your other classmates. Use a formal or informal style.

> Ana, I'd like you to meet Li.

> It's nice to meet you, Ana.

Useful Expressions		
	Introducing a person to someone else	**Responding to introductions**
formal ↑	Mr. Otani, I'd like to introduce you to Andres.	It's (very) nice to meet you. (It's) nice / good to meet you, too.
	Mr. Otani, I'd like you to meet Andres.	
↓ informal	Junko, this is Ricardo. Junko, meet Ricardo. Junko, Ricardo.	Nice / Good to meet you. You, too.
Speaking tip		
When you forget someone's name, it's best to be direct and say *I'm sorry, I'm terrible with names,* or *I'm sorry, I've forgotten your name.*		

5 GRAMMAR

A Turn to page 193. Complete the exercises. Then do **B–D** below.

The Simple Present Tense vs. the Present Continuous Tense	
I always **take** a shower in the morning. She**'s taking** a shower. Can she call you back?	Use the simple present to talk about habits, schedules, and facts. Use the present continuous to talk about actions that are happening right now.
I **live** in Taipei. (my permanent home) At the moment, I**'m living** in Taipei. (my home for now)	The present continuous can show that a situation is more temporary.
How many classes **are** you **taking** this term?	Use the present continuous to talk about actions happening in the extended present (nowadays).

B Read the sentences below. Circle the simple present tense verbs and underline the present continuous tense verbs. Then match each sentence to its usage on the right.

1. Sophia (is) my classmate.   a. describing a routine

2. She's living at home this term.   b. stating a truth or fact

3. She comes to school every day at 8:00.   c. happening right now

4. She's majoring in science.   d. happening in the extended present (nowadays)

5. We're studying together for a test right now.   e. suggesting a temporary situation

C Complete the sentences to make questions in the simple present or the present continuous. Use the verbs in the box.

> do   eat   have   ~~study~~   take   talk

1. A: Why _are you studying_ English now?

   B: I need it for work.

2. A: _____ any other classes this term?

   B: Yes, I am. Two business classes.

3. A: When _____ breakfast?

   B: Around 7:00, usually.

4. A: How many brothers and sisters _____?

   B: Four brothers and one sister.

5. A: What _____ on the weekends?

   B: I relax and hang out with friends.

6. A: Who _____ to right now?

   B: Alex.

D  Now take turns asking and answering the questions in **C** with a partner.

Harvard University

> Why are you studying English now?

> Well, I'm taking the TOEFL soon. I want to apply to Harvard University in the United States.

6 COMMUNICATION

A Take a sheet of paper and cut it into five strips.

On strips 1–3, write the following:

1. a routine you never change
2. an unusual habit
3. a general fact about yourself

On strips 4 and 5, write the following:

4. an activity you are doing these days
5. why you are studying English

B Give your papers to your instructor. He or she will mix up the papers and give you five new sentences.

1. I always get up at 5 AM.

2. I sometimes eat peanut butter and tomato sandwiches.

3. I have a twin brother.

4. I'm learning to play the guitar.

5. I'm studying English because it's my major.

C Talk to your classmates. Ask questions to find out who wrote each sentence.

D Tell the class an interesting fact you learned about one of your classmates.

1 VOCABULARY

A 🔄 Match a statement (1, 2, or 3) with a person above. Then ask a partner: What is each person doing? Why?

1. "I **have** track **practice** every day after school. I also **take** tennis **lessons** on the weekend."

2. "I'm **taking a class** to **prepare** for the university entrance **exam**. The class **meets** for three hours a day. It's a lot of work, but I need help to **pass** the test."

3. "Last term, I **failed** science. Now a **tutor** comes and helps me with my homework. This term, I'm **getting** a good **grade** in my science class!"

PASS ≠ FAIL

B 🔄 Complete the sentences with the blue words in **A**. Then check answers with a partner.

1. I can't go out with you. I _____HAVE_____ baseball _____PRACTICE_____ this afternoon.

2. Tyler never studies, so now he is _____GETTING_____ a bad _____GRADE_____ in all of his classes.

3. If I study really hard, I know I can _____PASS_____ the test!

4. This term, I'm _____TAKING_____ two business classes at City University.

5. Our English class _____MEETS_____ on Tuesdays and Thursdays.

6. To _____PREPARE_____ for tomorrow's class, please read pages 20 to 45.

7. My piano _____LESSONS_____ aren't long. They're only 30 minutes.

8. Liam _____FAILED_____ his math class, so he has to retake it next term.

9. Nico is a _____TUTOR_____. He helps students with their homework.

10. The _____EXAM_____ is this week, so I need to study.

Word Bank
Word Partnerships
have baseball / soccer / swim **practice**
take music / tennis **lessons**
take a(n) class / exam

C 🗣 Ask a partner the questions.

1. What classes are you taking now? When do they meet?
2. Are you taking any music or sports lessons?
3. How are you doing in your classes? Are you getting good grades?

2 LISTENING

a. He has practice in the morning only.

b. The camp lasts for a week.

c. At night, he stays in a dorm.

a. The class meets two times a week.

b. Students can work with a tutor.

c. The class is expensive.

a. The class is at a school in Singapore.

b. The class meets every day for four weeks.

c. Her teacher is Japanese.

A **Make predictions.** Look at the photos. Guess: What do people learn to do in each place?

B 🔊 **Listen for gist; Check predictions.** You will hear three people talking. Listen and number the pictures in the order you hear them (1, 2, or 3). CD 1 Track 6

C 🔊 **Listen for details.** Listen again. Below each photo, circle the answer that is not true. Then correct it. CD 1 Track 6

D 🔊 **Listen for details.** What are the benefits (good things) of taking each class? Listen again and write your answers below. CD 1 Track 6

1. Her score _____ WENT UP _____ 50 points.
2. She will know how to _____ MAKE THREE _____ beautiful cakes.
3. He will be a _____ BETTER PLAYER _____ next year.

E 🗣 Would you like to take any of these classes? Tell a partner.

3 READING

A **Understand the main idea.** Look at the words in the Word Bank. Then read the title and text below it. What is the main idea?

Word Bank
Opposites
fail (*v.*) ↔ succeed (*v.*)
failure (*n.*) ↔ success (*n.*)
successful (*adj.*)
give up (quit) ↔ keep trying

a. Sometimes it's best to give up.

b. When you fail, don't give up.

c. Careful people don't fail.

d. Some successful people give up.

B 🔲 **Read for details.** Work with a partner. Read about your person only. Then answer the questions below about him or her.

STUDENT A: Read about Black.

STUDENT B: Read about Lindsey Stirling.

1. What is the person's job?

2. What difficult things happened to the person?

3. What finally happened to the person? Was he or she successful?

C 🔲 **Summarize.** Ask your partner the questions in **B** about his or her person.

Listen and take notes. Then read about the other person. Check your partner's answers.

D 🔲 **Synthesize information.** Work with a partner. Answer the questions.

1. Look at the reading title. It is part of the expression *If at first you don't succeed, try, try again.* What does this expression mean? How are Black's and Lindsey Stirling's experiences an example of this expression?

2. Talk about a time you failed at something. When it happened, did you give up or keep trying? Did you learn anything?

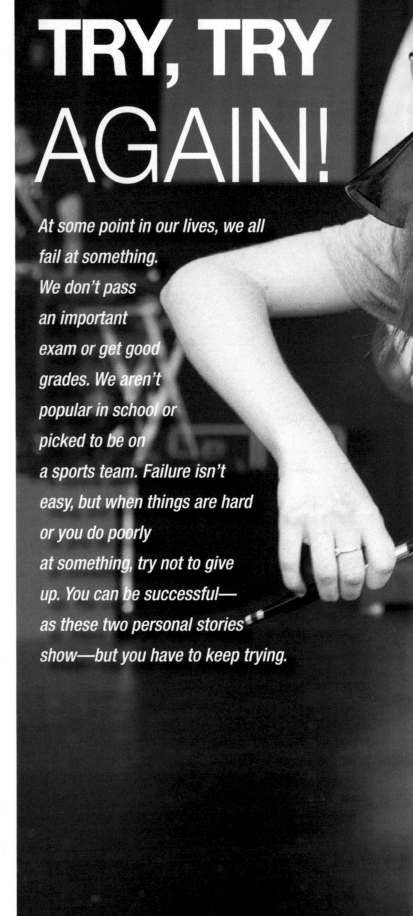

TRY, TRY AGAIN!

At some point in our lives, we all fail at something. We don't pass an important exam or get good grades. We aren't popular in school or picked to be on a sports team. Failure isn't easy, but when things are hard or you do poorly at something, try not to give up. You can be successful—as these two personal stories show—but you have to keep trying.

Black is a Japanese performance artist. Today he is a successful entertainer,[1] but as a teenager, his life was very different. In school, he was quiet and shy, and other boys bullied[2] him. People said to him, "Play a sport!" but Black wasn't good at sports. Then one day, Black bought a yo-yo and his life changed. At first, he couldn't do any tricks, but he didn't give up. He watched videos and practiced. In time, he became very good, and he decided to prepare for the World Yo-Yo Contest.[3] For four years, Black worked hard and practiced. Then, at age 18, he entered the contest, and he won. On that day, he was no longer a shy high school student. He was a world champion.[3]

Lindsey Stirling is an American musician. She mixes classical violin with dance music and hip-hop. As a child, Lindsey learned to play the violin. Her parents didn't have a lot of money, so she could only take lessons part time. Despite this, Lindsey practiced a lot, and she became very good. In high school, she started writing her own songs. Then at age 23, Lindsey was on a popular TV talent show. She did well, but in the end, she lost. The judges said she wasn't interesting enough. Lindsey was very sad, but she didn't give up. She kept trying. In time, she made a music video and her first album. Later, she won an important music award. Today, she has one of the most popular channels on YouTube.

[1]An *entertainer* is someone like an actor, musician, dancer, or singer.
[2]If someone *bullies* you, they try to hurt you or make you afraid.
[3]A *contest* is a game that people try to win. The winner is the *champion*.

4 GRAMMAR

A Turn to page 194. Complete the exercises. Then do **B–D** below.

Review of the Simple Past Tense		
	Yes / No questions	**Answers**
With be	Were you in class today?	Yes, I was. / No, I wasn't.
With other verbs	Did you pass the test?	Yes, I did. / No, I didn't.
	Wh- questions	**Answers**
With be	Where were you last night?	(I was) at my friend's house.
With other verbs	When did you meet your girlfriend?	(We met) last year.

calligraphy

B Complete the profile with the simple past tense form of the verbs in parentheses. Then take turns reading the profile aloud with a partner.

Apple cofounder Steve Jobs (1. not graduate) _____ from college. Jobs (2. be) _____ a smart guy, but his school (3. be) _____ expensive, and he (4. not have) _____ enough money to go. So he (5. leave) _____ college, and he (6. take) _____ a calligraphy class instead.

When his parents (7. hear) _____ this, they (8. be) _____ worried. "Why calligraphy?" his parents (9. ask) _____. "What can you do with that?" Jobs (10. not be) _____ sure. The class (11. not help) _____ him get a job, but years later, it (12. help) _____ him in another way. Jobs (13. use) _____ ideas from his calligraphy class to create Apple's famous computer fonts.

C Work with a partner. Follow the steps below.

1. On your own, write three *Yes / No* and three *Wh-* simple past tense questions about Jobs on a piece of paper.
2. Cover the profile in **B**.
3. Take turns asking and answering the questions with a partner.

> Did Steve Jobs graduate from college?

> No, he didn't.

> Why not?

Steve Jobs

D Think of a famous person from the past. Your partner asks you five past tense questions and tries to guess the person. Then switch roles and repeat.

5 WRITING

When I was fourteen, I couldn't swim. As a child, I was afraid of the water, so I never learned. Usually, this wasn't a problem, but in the summer, things were different. All of my friends went to the public pool on hot days. I went, too, but I had to watch them have fun. Finally, I decided to take swimming lessons at a place near my house. The class met every day. At first, I was very nervous, but I didn't give up. I practiced and, by the end, I was a good swimmer.

I couldn't... well, but I learned to.
dance
drive
play a sport
play an instrument
ride a bike
speak a language
speak in public
my idea: _____

A Read the paragraph. Then answer the questions with a partner.

1. What couldn't the person do?
2. Why was this a problem?
3. How did the person learn?
4. Was the person successful?

B Think about something you couldn't do, but learned to do. Answer the questions in **A** about yourself. Then use your ideas and the example above to help you write your own paragraph. Remember to use the correct simple past tense verbs.

C Exchange papers with a partner. Circle any mistakes in your partner's paper. Answer the questions in **A** about your partner. Are your experiences similar or different?

6 COMMUNICATION

A Work in a small group. Read the questions below. Then add one simple past tense *Yes / No* question and one simple past tense *Wh-* question.

In high school...

1. were you a good or bad student?
2. did you play any sports?
3. what was your favorite subject?
4. what did you do for fun?
5. _____
6. _____

B Think about your answers to the questions in **A**. Make some notes.

> I was a good student in high school. I got good grades and...

C Get into a group of four people. Follow the steps below.

1. One person begins. Choose a question in **A**.

   Speaker: Answer the question. Talk for one minute without stopping.

   Listeners: Listen to the speaker. Then answer the questions below. If the group answers *yes* to both questions, the speaker gets a point.

   • Did the speaker keep talking for one minute without stopping a lot?
   • Could you understand the person clearly?

2. Repeat step 1 with a different speaker. Continue taking turns for 25 minutes. The winner: the person with the most points.

2 LET'S EAT!

Look at the photo. Answer the questions.

1 What food is in the photo? Do you like it?

2 Is this food healthy or not? Why?

3 What are three of your favorite foods? Why do you like them?

UNIT GOALS

1 Describe foods and how they are prepared

2 Make and respond to suggestions

3 Describe a healthy diet and lifestyle

4 Rate a restaurant and explain why you like it

A man presents ice cream at an ice cream shop in Buenos Aires, Argentina.

1 VIDEO Frozen, Fresh, or Canned?

A 🔲 Look at these words that describe food. Use your dictionary to look up any you don't know. Which kind of food is the healthiest to eat? Tell a partner.

fresh　　*frozen*　　*canned*

Word Bank
farmers' market = a place where local farmers sell their products directly to the public
pick = to break a fruit or vegetable off a plant or tree and collect it
salt = white powder used to improve the taste of food

B ▶ Watch the beginning of the video with the sound off. What kind of food do you see? Check (✓) your answers.

☐ fresh food　　　　☐ frozen food　　　　☐ canned food

SOUR = AMARGO
BITTER = AZEDO

C ▶ Watch again. Write one or two words to complete each sentence.

1. Frozen and canned vegetables are ____GOOD FOR____ you, too, because most are packed (put in bags and cans) right after picking.

2. But beware (be careful) of the ____SALT____ in ____CANNED____ veggies.

3. ____DON'T____ overboil vegetables.

D 🔲 How often do you eat fresh fruit and vegetables? How about frozen or canned ones? Tell a partner.

2 VOCABULARY

A Read about a snack food called *paletas*. Find two words that mean the food is good and circle them. Would you like to try this food? Why or why not?

Paletas are **delicious**, **frozen** fruit snacks.

Their name comes from *palo* or "stick."

They are made with water or juice and fresh fruit, so they are **sweet**.

Sometimes chili pepper is added, so they can be **spicy**, too.

These **tasty** treats are a popular street food in Mexico.

paletas

B Think of a popular street food. Make notes. Use words from the Word Bank below.

Name of the food: _CALDEIRADA DE FRUTOS DO MAR_

Taste: _DELICIOUS_

Preparation: _OCTOPUS, SCHRIMP, FISH_
ONION, TOMATO,

ℹ️ You can add *y* to many nouns to make adjectives meaning "full of (something)."
juicy oily salty spicy tasty
OLEOSO
SUCULENTO(A)

a banh mi sandwich

C 💬 Tell a partner about your food. Use your notes from **B**.

> Banh mi sandwiches are tasty. My favorite kind is made with grilled pork, cucumbers, and carrots. They are a popular street food in Vietnam.

Word Bank
How foods taste
spicy ↔ mild LEMON
sweet ↔ sour / bitter AMORGO
delicious / tasty / yummy ↔ awful / terrible
How foods are prepared
baked, fried, frozen, grilled, STEAMED

RAW = CRUA

3 LISTENING

A 🔄 **Make predictions.** Look at the four photos below. What do you think each food tastes like? Tell your partner.

B 🔊 **Check predictions.** Listen to the beginning of Bill and Marta's conversation. Complete the information about the food. **CD 1 Track 8**

Foods from the (1.) _SOUTHERN_ United States

grits

(3.) _FRIED_ green tomatoes

(2.) _FRIED_ chicken

(4.) Mississippi _MUD_ pie
↳ _LAMA, BARRO_

C 🔊 **Listen for details.** Listen to the rest of the conversation. Write the words used to describe the foods. Then circle the food above that Marta *didn't* like. Why didn't she like it? **CD 1 Track 9**

1. The chicken was _DELICIOUS_.

2. The grits tasted like oatmeal with a strong _BUTTERY_ flavor.

3. The tomatoes were _oily_, but they went _well_ with the chicken and grits.

4. The dessert was a thick _CHOCOLATE_ pie. It was too _SWEET_.

D 🔄 **Talk with a partner.** Do these four foods sound good to you? Why or why not? Is your hometown (or region) famous for a special food? Describe it.

E 🔊 **Pronunciation: Sentence stress and rhythm.** Read these complaints. Then say the sentences. Underline the stressed syllables or words in each sentence. Then listen and check your answers. **CD 1 Track 10**

1. The dinner was cold.

2. The chicken was dry.

3. The grits were terrible.

4. The lemon pie was too sour.

WORLD LINK

Go online and find one more food from the southern United States. Describe it. Would you like to try it?

4 SPEAKING

A 🔊 Listen to the conversation. Then answer the questions.
CD 1 Track 11

1. What are Jose and Jill going to eat for dinner?

2. How do Jose and Jill make and respond to suggestions? Underline the words.

JOSE: So, Jill, where do you want to go to dinner tonight?

JILL: I don't know. Why don't we go to the pizza place on the corner?

JOSE: Pizza again? I don't really feel like it.

JILL: OK, how about Thai food instead?

JOSE: Fine with me. Where do you want to go?

JILL: Well, Thai House is near here. And there's another place—The Thai Cafe—but it's downtown.

JOSE: Thai House is closer. Let's go there.

JILL: Sounds good!

B 🗣 Practice the conversation with a partner.

SPEAKING STRATEGY

C 🗣 Study the Useful Expressions. Then complete the dialogs below with a partner. Sometimes more than one answer is possible.

1. A: ___Let's___ stop at that cafe for coffee.
   B: Good ___idea___!

2. A: What time do you want to meet in the morning?
   B: ___Why don't we___ meet at 7:00?
   A: That's a little early. ___How about___ meeting at 8:00 instead?
   B: That's ___fine___ with me. See you then.

3. A: What do you want to do today?
   B: ___How about___ going to the beach?
   A: I don't ___really want___ to. ___Let's___ see a movie instead.
   B: OK, ___sounds___ good.

Useful Expressions			
Making suggestions			**Responding to suggestions**
Statements			Good / Great idea!
Let's	have	Thai food for dinner.	(That) sounds good (to me).
Questions			(That's) fine with me.
Why don't we	have	Thai food for dinner?	I don't really want to.
How about	having		I don't really feel like it.
Speaking tip			
When rejecting a suggestion, it's common to give an explanation: *I don't really feel like it. I'm too tired.*			

Why don't we go to Parr's Steakhouse for lunch?

That's a great idea!

I don't really feel like steak. How about having Indian food instead?

D 👥 Get into a group of three and do the following:

1. On your own: think of two good restaurants.

2. Suggest one of the restaurants to your partners. They can accept or refuse. If a person refuses, he or she should say why and suggest another restaurant.

3. Change roles and repeat steps 1 and 2 until each student makes a suggestion.

5 GRAMMAR

A Turn to page 195. Complete the exercises. Then do **B** and **C** below.

The Comparative Form of Adjectives			
One syllable	**Two syllables**	**Three or more syllables**	**Irregular forms**
old → old**er**	quiet → quiet**er**	comfortable → **more** comfortable	good → **better**
nice → nice**r**	spicy → spic**ier**		bad → **worse**
big → big**ger**	famous → **more** famous		

Note: The comparative form of *well* (an adverb) is *better*.

B Use the words to make questions with *which* in the comparative form.

1. tasty / restaurant food / your own cooking

   Which is tastier, restaurant food or your own cooking?

2. go well with steak / french fries / a baked potato

   _____

3. good / drinking tea / drinking coffee

   _____

4. fun / eating out with family / getting fast food with friends

   _____

5. bad / arriving 30 minutes early to a dinner party / being 30 minutes late

   _____

> **i** We typically use *which*, not *what*, when there is a smaller, more defined number of choices.
> *What did you have for dessert last night?*
> *Which pie did you bake for the party, the chocolate one or the lemon one?*

C 🔄 Ask and answer the questions in **B** with a partner. Give reasons for your answers.

> Which is tastier, restaurant food or your own cooking?

> My own cooking is tastier. I'm a pretty good cook!

6 COMMUNICATION

A 🔄 Look at the pictures of Veronica's Restaurant. Talk with a partner about the changes you see. Use the adjectives in the box to help you.

bad	comfortable	new
bright	dirty	nice
busy	good	old
cheerful	messy	sad
clean		

the old Veronica's

The old Veronica's was dirty.
The new Veronica's is cleaner.

the new Veronica's

B 🔄 With a partner, make a twenty-second radio advertisement for the new Veronica's using your ideas from **A**. Write your ideas below. Then practice the announcement aloud.

_____

_____

_____

_____

C 👥 Present your radio advertisement to the class. Whose was the best? Why?

Come and see the new Veronica's!
It's brighter and better than ever.

Mexico, Japan, Cameroon, and Greece. How are these countries similar? In her book *The Jungle Effect*, Dr. Daphne Miller says these places have some of the world's healthiest people. Why? Their traditional diets have important health benefits, says Dr. Miller. The things they eat and drink increase their energy and protect them from dangerous illnesses.

Dr. Miller says a healthy diet and lifestyle are important. She says we should:

- eat more fresh fruit, vegetables, and fish.
- cut back on red meat and instant (pre-made) foods. Only eat these sometimes.
- completely eliminate unhealthy habits like smoking.
- get plenty (lots) of exercise.

a table of traditional Greek food

1 VOCABULARY

A Read the information above. Then answer the questions with a partner.

1. How are the four countries mentioned similar? Why are their traditional diets special?
2. Would Dr. Miller agree with these statements? Why or why not?

   Eat more hamburgers.   *Don't smoke at all.*   *Going to the gym once a month is enough.*

B Take the quiz. Circle T for *True* and F for *False*. Choose the answers that are true for you.

1. I need to cut back on red meat in my diet.   T   (F)
2. I eat plenty of fruit and vegetables.   T   (F)
3. I get plenty of exercise.   T   (F)
4. I have one or two bad habits.   T   (F)

C Do you have a healthy diet and lifestyle? Why or why not? Use your answers in **B** to tell a partner.

> I have a healthy diet and lifestyle.
> I get plenty of exercise, and I eat...

2 LISTENING

Tadka dal, a spicy traditional **dish** (food) from India, has many health benefits.

Today, more people worldwide eat **fast food**, and health problems are increasing.

A Look at the photos. Which is healthier: tadka dal or fast food?

B **Make predictions.** You will hear two people talking about the Slow Food Movement. Guess: Which idea(s) (a–d) do its members believe are true? Circle the idea(s). Explain your guesses to a partner.

People should _____.

   a. not eat fast or instant foods

   b. grow food slowly and carefully

   c. not eat meat

   d. learn to cook their own meals

Word Bank
movement = a group of people with the same beliefs
member = part of a group

C **Check predictions.** Listen and check the correct answer(s) in **B**. CD 1 Track 12

D **Listen for details.** Read the sentences. Then listen again and circle *True* or *False*. CD 1 Track 12

Alessandro Moretti thinks…

1. most Slow Food members are Italian.	True	**False**
2. eating a slow food diet is hard for busy people.	True	**False**
3. a slow food diet has health benefits.	**True**	False
4. many people today don't know how to cook.	**True**	False
5. you should learn your grandparents' recipes.	**True**	False

E Discuss the questions with a partner.

1. Do you like the Slow Food Movement's ideas? Why or why not?

2. Do you eat a lot of fast food? Can you cook any traditional dishes?

THE HEALTHIEST LIFESTYLE IN THE WORLD?

3 READING

A 🔄 **Skim for the main idea; Make predictions.** Look quickly at the title, picture, and article. Then try to guess the correct answers below. Explain your ideas to a partner.

1. The reading is mainly about _____.

   a. people from around the world

   b. healthcare for older people

   c. a group of people from Japan

   d. older people in the United States

2. What is unusual about these people?

   a. Most of them are women.

   b. Many live to age 100 or older.

   c. They have the spiciest food in the world.

   d. There are only 100 of them.

B **Check predictions.** Now read the article and check your answers in **A**.

C **Scan for information.** Read quickly through the article again and complete the chart below. You have two minutes.

Okinawan Centenarians

What they eat	What they drink
fruits	water
vegetables	green tea
fish	**How they relax**
tofu	SIT QUIETLY
How they exercise	RELAX
GARDENING	BREATH DEEPLY
WALKING	SPEND TIME WITH FAMILY AND FRIENDS

D 🔄 Answer the questions with a partner.

1. Why do Okinawans live so long? Give reasons from the reading.

2. Do people in your country have healthy lifestyles? Use the chart in **C** to give examples.

An 84-year-old Okinawan man does yoga daily on the beach in Naha.

In many countries around the world, people are living longer than before. People have healthier lifestyles, and healthcare is better, too.

Okinawa is an island off the coast of Japan. The people on Okinawa, the Okinawans, may have the longest lives and healthiest lifestyles in the world.

Researchers did a study. They started by looking at city and town birth records from 1879. They didn't expect to find many centenarians (hundred-year-olds) in the records, so they were very surprised to find so many old and healthy people living in Okinawa. The United States, for example, has ten centenarians per 100,000 people. In Okinawa, there are 34 centenarians per 100,000 people!

What is the Okinawans' secret? First, they eat a healthy diet that includes fresh fruits and vegetables. They also eat fish and tofu and drink plenty of water and green tea. But researchers think that the Okinawans have other healthy habits as well. They don't do hard exercise such as weightlifting or jogging. Instead, they prefer relaxing activities like gardening and walking. They sit quietly and relax their minds by breathing deeply. They also spend time with family members and friends.

4 GRAMMAR

A Turn to page 196. Complete the exercises. Then do **B–D** below.

The Superlative Form of Adjectives			
One syllable	**Two syllables**	**Three or more syllables**	**Irregular forms**
old → **the** old**est** large → **the** larg**est** big → **the** big**gest**	quiet → **the** quiet**est** spicy → **the** spic**iest** famous → **the most** famous	comfortable → **the most** comfortable important → **the most** important relaxing → **the most** relaxing	good → **the best** bad → **the worst**

B Complete the restaurant profile with the superlative form of the adjectives in parentheses.

Are you looking for an interesting place to have a meal? One of (1. unusual) _____ places in

the world is Ithaa Restaurant in the Maldives, where you eat underwater! Ithaa is one of

(2. trendy) _____ restaurants in the world. For many, it is also (3. popular) _____

place to visit in the Maldives. It's not (4. cheap) _____ restaurant, but it's

(5. good) _____ way to see the island's coral and fish. The food is good, too. "I had

(6. delicious) _____ meal of my life," says one visitor to the restaurant. His girlfriend agrees.

"It was (7. weird) _____ but (8. interesting) _____ dining experience I ever had!"

C Answer the questions with a partner.

1. Why is the restaurant in **B** unusual?

2. Why do people like it?

3. Does it sound interesting to you? Why or why not?

bad	cheap	romantic
boring	noisy	trendy

D Work with a partner. Use the adjectives in the box to talk about restaurants and cafes you know.

> The Left Bank is the noisiest cafe in this area.

5 WRITING

Amazon Sun

Amazon Sun is the best Brazilian restaurant in this city. The food is delicious, the service is friendly, and the prices are moderate. One of the tastiest dishes on the menu is the feijoada completa—a traditional dish of meat, beans, and Brazilian spices. It's excellent!

A 🔁 Read the restaurant review and complete the notes about the place. Then ask and answer questions about the restaurant with a partner.

Restaurant name: _____

Type of food: _____

Prices: expensive / moderate / cheap

Service: _____

Best dish: _____

Is it an expensive restaurant?

No, the prices are moderate.

B Choose a restaurant you know and make some notes about it. Use the model in **A**. Then use your notes to write your own restaurant review.

C 🔁 Exchange your writing with a partner. Read his or her review.

1. Are there any mistakes? If yes, circle them.
2. Complete the notes in **A** about your partner's place.
3. Give the review back to your partner. Do you want to try his or her restaurant? Why?

6 COMMUNICATION

A 🔁 With a partner, create a menu for a new restaurant or coffee shop. Divide the menu into sections (appetizers, main dishes, drinks, desserts). Include prices.

B Post your menus for the class to see. Then walk around and learn about the restaurants in your class. Take notes.

C 🔁 Work with your partner. Answer the questions about the restaurants in your class.

1. Which restaurant is the cheapest?
2. Which is the most expensive?
3. Which has the healthiest food?
4. Which is the best? Why?

Why don't we try Noodle Barn?

D 🔁 Choose a restaurant from the class list. Suggest eating there with your partner. Use the Useful Expressions on page 21.

Sounds good. I love ramen!

3 MYSTERIES

African baobab trees can live to be thousands of years old. Scientists still don't understand why some trees live so long.

Frane Selak's car plunged off of a mountain road, but he survived!

1 VIDEO The Luckiest Unlucky Man to Ever Live

lucky

unlucky

survived

accidents

A Frane Selak is called the "luckiest unlucky man to ever live." Complete the information about Frane with the words in the box.

Frane had many _____. That was _____. But he _____. That was _____.

B ▶ Read the question and answers on the left. Watch the video. Then put the events in order from 1 to 7.

What unlucky things happened to Frane?

_____ His car went off a mountain road.

_____ He was in a plane crash.

_____ He was in a bus crash.

___1___ He was in a train crash.

_____ His car burst into flames.

_____ A bus hit him.

_____ His car burst into flames—again.

Why was he lucky?

a. A door blew off, and Frane landed in a haystack.

b. Frane only broke his arm.

c. Frane jumped free.

d. Four people were killed but not Frane.

e. Frane survived.

f. Frane jumped out and landed in a tree.

g. Frane survived (but with less hair).

C ▶ Why was Frane lucky each time? Watch again. Match each event (1–7) with a reason (a–g).

D 🔁 Answer the questions with a partner.

1. What lucky thing happened to Frane in 2003?

2. Why is Frane the luckiest unlucky man to ever live? Explain in your own words.

32 UNIT 3 • Mysteries

2 VOCABULARY

A Answer the questions.

1. **Lucky** people have good things happen to them. Are you lucky?
   Why or why not? _____
   _____

2. Do you ever do things (like wear a lucky color) for **good luck**? Do
   you do anything to avoid **bad luck**? _____
   _____

3. Write down some notes about something good that has happened
   to you. Did you do it **on purpose** (plan it), or did it happen by
   chance (by luck)? _____
   _____

4. Do you make decisions based more on **facts** (true information about
   something) or on your **intuition** (feelings)? Explain. _____
   _____

5. What lucky objects do you know about? Do you own a lucky object? Where do
   you keep it? How does it help? _____
   _____

6. *It's better to be lucky than to be smart.* Do you agree or disagree with this
   statement? Why? _____
   _____

Word Bank
Opposites
lucky ↔ unlucky
good luck ↔ bad luck
(do something) **on purpose** ↔ (happen) **by chance**
facts ↔ **intuition**

B 🔁 Ask and answer the questions in **A** with a partner.

> Do you do anything
> to avoid bad luck?

> People say that stepping on a crack in the
> sidewalk is bad luck, so I don't do it.

Some people think that seeing a rainbow is a lucky sign.

3 LISTENING

A 🔊 **Pronunciation: Dropped syllables.** Say these words. Look up any words that you don't know. Then listen and repeat. **CD 1 Track 14**

1. interesting	2. generally	3. everywhere	4. finally
in'tres ting	*gen' ra lly*	*ev' ry where*	*fin' lly*

B 🔄 Read the sentences. Which one do you agree with more? Tell a partner.

1. Some people are just lucky in life.   2. You can learn to be lucky in life.

C 🔊 **Listen for gist.** You will hear a talk about psychologist Professor Wiseman and his research on luck. Listen. Which sentence in **B** (1 or 2) does he believe? Circle it. **CD 1 Track 15**

> **Word Bank**
>
> Sometimes, words have different meanings depending on how they are used.
>
> ***take a chance*** *chance* = risk
>
> ***by chance*** *chance* = luck
>
> ***increase your chances***
> *chances* = opportunities

D 🔊 **Make predictions; Listen for details.** Read the statements below. Do they describe lucky people or unlucky people? Make predictions. Then listen and check your answers. **CD 1 Track 16**

Write *L* for "lucky people." Write *U* for "unlucky people."

Write *B* if it is true for <u>both</u> types of people.

ℹ️ Notice as you listen: The speaker uses *on the other hand* to introduce a contrasting (or an opposite) idea.

1. _____ They spend more time alone.

2. _____ They don't like surprises.

3. _____ They have a lot of friends.

4. _____ They make decisions.

5. _____ They follow their intuition.

6. _____ They have bad experiences.

7. _____ They try to find the good in a bad situation.

E 🔄 Answer the questions with a partner.

1. Was your answer in **B** the same as Professor Wiseman's? Do you agree with him? Why or why not?

2. Look at the statements in **D**. Which ones are true for you?

Many cultures have lucky charms. The *maneki-neko* is popular in Japan.

WORLD LINK

Go online and learn about a lucky charm that is used in another culture. Tell a partner about it.

SPEAKING

(handwritten top notes) most likely = {muito provável / provavelmente!

most likely NOT = mais provável que não

SURE = 100%
MOST LIKELY = 90/99%
PROBABLY = 85/99%
MAYBE/PERHAPS = 50%
UNDER 50% = is negative idea
MOST LIKELY it's NOT
I DOUBT...

A 🔊 Nico and Sandra are talking about a news article. Listen and answer the questions. **CD 1 Track 17**

1. What did a woman in New York City do?

2. What is she going to do now?

SANDRA: Anything interesting in today's news?

NICO: Yeah, I'm reading about a woman in New York City. She just won $25,000.

SANDRA: That's a lot of money. Did she win the lottery?

NICO: No, she guessed the correct number of candies in a jar.

SANDRA: Really? How many were there?

NICO: 7,954.

SANDRA: Wow. That was a lucky guess!

NICO: I know. I doubt that I could do that!

SANDRA: So, what's she going to do with the money?

NICO: I don't know. Perhaps she'll go on a vacation or use it for school.

How many candies are in this jar?   *(handwritten)* I BET = I THINK

B ♻ Practice the conversation with a partner.

SPEAKING STRATEGY

C On the lines below, write two things about yourself that are true. Write one thing that is a lie.

1. *(handwritten)* I will most likely have dinner tonight.

2. *(handwritten)* Maybe you want to take a break?

3. *(handwritten)* I will probably learn two languages here in Orlando.

Useful Expressions: Talking about Possibility	
Saying something is likely	
I bet (that)	Marco plays the drums.
Marco probably	plays the drums.
Maybe / Perhaps	Marco plays the drums.
Saying something is *not* likely	
I doubt (that)	Marco plays the drums.
Speaking tip	
You can use *Are you sure?* to ask if a person is certain about something.	

D 🎲 Get into a group of three or four people. Follow the steps below.

1. One person tells the group his or her sentences.

2. The others...

   • ask the speaker questions to find out which sentence is a lie.

   • use the Useful Expressions to discuss their ideas.

   • guess which sentence is a lie. If you guess correctly, you get a point.

3. Change roles and repeat steps 1 and 2.

I bet Marco plays the drums. I saw him with a pair of drumsticks one time.

Are you sure they were his drumsticks? Maybe they belong to someone else.

(handwritten) MOST LIKELY, I AM GOING TO ITALY NEXT YEAR.

(handwritten) I probably passed the exam.

(handwritten) I bet = I think → you believe it's true!

5 GRAMMAR

A Turn to page 197. Complete the exercise. Then do **B–D** below.

Stative Verbs				
Thinking verbs	**Having verbs**	**Feeling verbs**	**Sensing verbs**	**Other verbs**
believe	_____	appreciate	_____	seem
know	have	_____	see	look
_____	_____	_____	_____	mean
_____		love	taste	cost
				need

B Look at the stative verbs in the box below. Then add them to the chart at the top of the page.

| belong | hate | hear | like | own | smell | think | understand |

C Read the story below. Circle the correct form of each verb. Use the present continuous wherever possible.

> Winning the lottery—to most people, it (1.) seems / is seeming like great luck. Unfortunately, for the winners, it's often the opposite. Ian Walters, for example, won a million dollars in a lottery five years ago. "Suddenly (2.) you have / you're having a lot of money," he explains. "(3.) You think / You're thinking it will last forever, and you spend it quickly." And then one day, the money is gone. "These days, (4.) I live / I'm living with my sister temporarily, and (5.) I work / I'm working in a small cafe. (6.) I don't own / I'm not owning a car because I can't afford it," says Ian. "It's not so bad, though. I now (7.) know / am knowing that money can't buy happiness. (8.) I appreciate / I'm appreciating each day. And (9.) I look forward / I'm looking forward to the future."

> **i** Stative verbs are not usually used in the present continuous tense.

D Answer the questions with a partner.

1. *Winning the lottery seems like good luck.* Do you agree with this statement?
2. Do you think money can buy happiness?
3. Do you need a certain amount of money to live?
4. What do you do to appreciate every day?

6 COMMUNICATION

A 🔁 Read the story. Then look at the photo. Without looking back at the story, answer these questions with a partner.

1. Who is Corina Sanchez?

2. What happened to Corina at around 12:00?

3. What happened to her son at around the same time?

4. How did Corina know?

On the morning of February 19, Corina Sanchez said goodbye to her husband and 17-year-old son and went to work. "It was a normal day," Corina remembers.

She went to lunch at the usual time: 12:00. Suddenly, she started to feel terrible. "I had a strong pain in my chest—near my heart," says Corina. "The pain came and went quickly. It was very strange."

Two hours later, Corina got a phone call with some bad news. Her son was in a car accident. Luckily, he wasn't hurt badly. The time of the accident? 12:02 PM.

B 🔁 Discuss the questions with a partner.

1. How did Corina know that something was wrong?

2. Some people think that mothers have special abilities. Do you believe in a "mother's intuition"?

C Think of a time when you had intuition about a situation or when something strange happened to you or someone you know. Complete the chart with your notes.

Who is the story about?	
What happened?	

D 🔁 Tell your story to a partner.

Why do we dream?

Everyone dreams, but scientists can't figure out why. Below are two explanations

"Our team is investigating the connection between dreams and our health.
Dreams might help us deal with stress. After we sleep and dream, we feel better."

"We have a different theory. Maybe dreams are just images in our minds.
We dream because the brain is 'cleaning out' unused information when we sleep."

Both ideas make sense, but for now, there's no proof for either one.
The only way to solve this mystery is to do more research.

1 VOCABULARY

A Look at the photo and the question *Why do we dream?* Think of answers with a partner.

B Take turns reading the information above with a partner. Then match the words in blue with a definition below. Some words have the same definition.

Understand →

Word or Phrase	Definition
figure out,	to find an answer to a question or problem
theory,	a guess or idea
investigate	to study something closely
make sense	to be logical or understandable
proof	facts that show that something is true

C Answer the questions with a partner. Use your ideas from **A** to explain your answers.

1. What are the two theories about dreams?

2. Do scientists have proof for either idea?

3. In your opinion, which explanation makes more sense?

Word Bank
Word Partnerships
have / need / there's (no) **proof**
have a **theory**

2 LISTENING

Some people think that more people act in a strange or dangerous way when the moon is full.

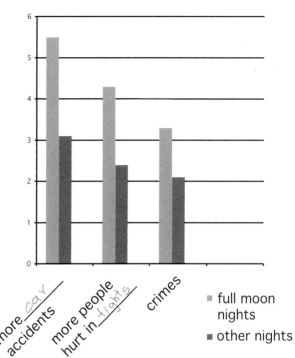

more ~~car~~ accidents   more people hurt in ~~fights~~   crimes

- full moon nights
- other nights

A ⟳ **Make predictions.** Look at the photo and the graph. Read the information. Then answer the questions with a partner.

1. What do some people think about the full moon?
2. Look at the graph. What do you think it's showing?

B 🔊 **Use visual aids; Listen for details.** You are going to hear a news report. **CD 1 Track 18**

1. Listen and complete the graph in **A**. Write one word in each blank.
2. What are city officials planning to do? Write your answer.

_____

C 🔊 **Listen for a speaker's opinion; Listen for details.** Read the questions and answers. Then listen and check (✓) *Yes* or *No* and complete the chart. **CD 1 Track 19**

	Does the moon affect our behavior?	**What's the person's theory?**
The woman	☑ Yes ☐ No	The moon affects the ___oceans___. Maybe it affects ___people___, too.
The man	☐ Yes ☑ No	On full moon nights, there's more ___light___, so more people ___go out___.

D ⟳ Answer the questions with a partner.

1. What do you think? Can the moon change our behavior?
2. Can you think of any other explanations for the higher crime and accident rates?

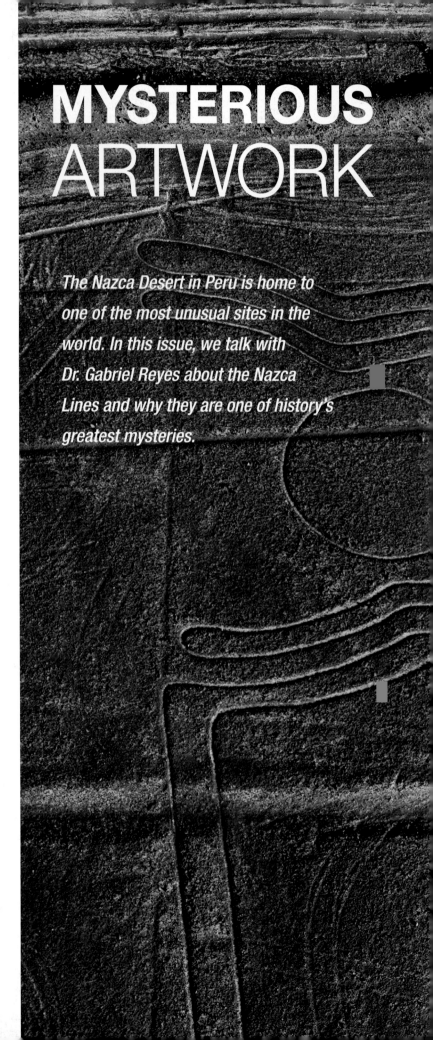

3 READING

A **Make predictions; Scan for details.** Look at the title and photo and answer the questions below. Then look quickly though the article to check your answers.

1. What do you think the drawing in the photo is?
2. Who do you think made it?

B **Identify main ideas.** Read the passage. Then write the questions below in the correct places in the interview. Two questions are extra.

How did they make the lines?

What was the purpose of the lines?

How do the local people feel about the lines?

What exactly are the Nazca Lines?

Can anyone visit the Nazca Lines?

Who made the ground drawings?

C **Read for details.** The statements below are wrong. Change them so that they are correct. Underline the sentence(s) in the interview that helped you make your changes.

1. The lines are small; you can only see them by looking closely at the ground.
2. North Americans probably created the lines in the year 1500.
3. It was probably difficult for people to make the lines without simple tools.
4. The Nazca Lines definitely were a calendar, say scientists.

D ⟳ Look at the four questions in the interview. Take turns asking and answering them with a partner. When you answer a question, use your own words. Try not to look back at the article.

MYSTERIOUS ARTWORK

The Nazca Desert in Peru is home to one of the most unusual sites in the world. In this issue, we talk with Dr. Gabriel Reyes about the Nazca Lines and why they are one of history's greatest mysteries.

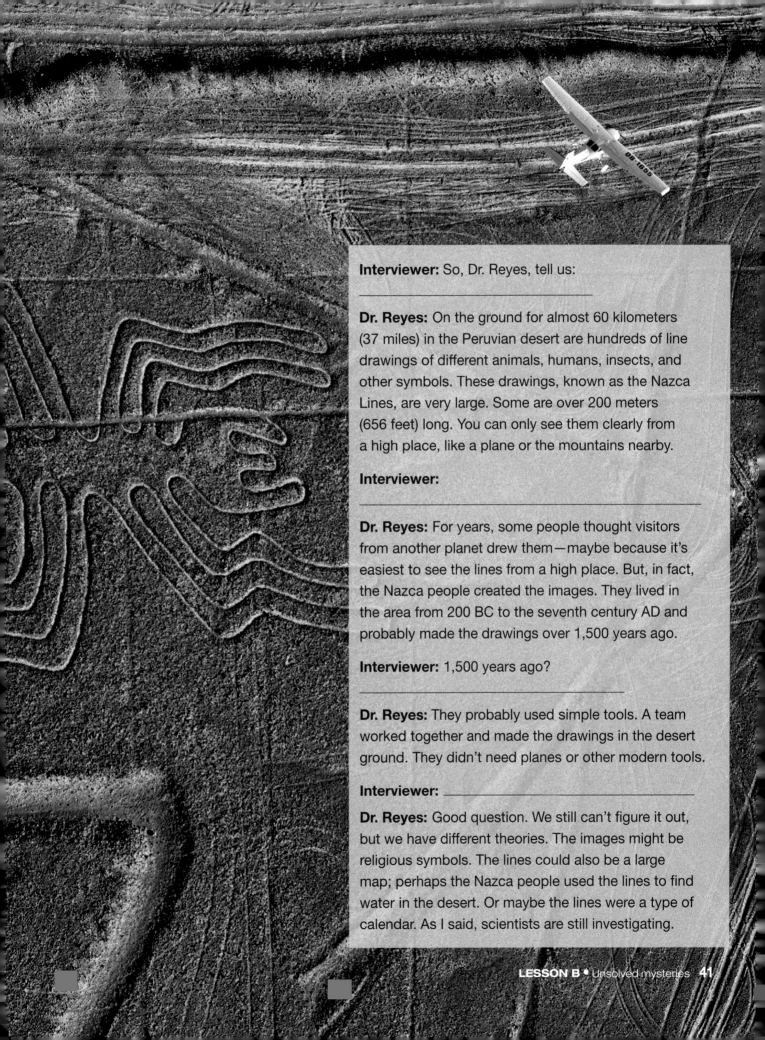

Interviewer: So, Dr. Reyes, tell us:

_____

Dr. Reyes: On the ground for almost 60 kilometers (37 miles) in the Peruvian desert are hundreds of line drawings of different animals, humans, insects, and other symbols. These drawings, known as the Nazca Lines, are very large. Some are over 200 meters (656 feet) long. You can only see them clearly from a high place, like a plane or the mountains nearby.

Interviewer:

_____

Dr. Reyes: For years, some people thought visitors from another planet drew them—maybe because it's easiest to see the lines from a high place. But, in fact, the Nazca people created the images. They lived in the area from 200 BC to the seventh century AD and probably made the drawings over 1,500 years ago.

Interviewer: 1,500 years ago?

_____

Dr. Reyes: They probably used simple tools. A team worked together and made the drawings in the desert ground. They didn't need planes or other modern tools.

Interviewer: _____

Dr. Reyes: Good question. We still can't figure it out, but we have different theories. The images might be religious symbols. The lines could also be a large map; perhaps the Nazca people used the lines to find water in the desert. Or maybe the lines were a type of calendar. As I said, scientists are still investigating.

4 GRAMMAR

A Turn to page 198. Complete the exercises. Then do **B** and **C** below.

Modals of Present Possibility			
Subject	**Modal**	**Main verb**	
The Loch Ness Monster	**may / might / could**	be	real. Maybe it's a large animal.
	can't		real. There are no sea monsters.

Questions and short answers		
With be	Is the Loch Ness Monster real?	It **may / might / could** be.
With other verbs	Does the full moon affect us?	It **may / might / could**.

B Complete the dialogs with a modal and a verb, if needed. Sometimes, more than one answer is possible. Then ask and answer the questions with a partner.

1. A: Does life exist on other planets?

   B: It _____. There are billions of planets. We _____ be the only intelligent life.

2. A: Worldwide, millions of bees are dying. Scientists can't figure out why. What's happening?

   B: Pesticides _____ be killing the bees. But it _____ be climate change, too.

3. A: Are ghosts real?

   B: Sure, they _____. A lot of people see them.

   C: No, they _____. There's no scientific proof for them.

Word Bank
pesticide = a chemical used to kill insects

C Ask the questions in **B** with a partner again. This time, give and explain your own opinion.

5 WRITING

A Read the paragraph. Answer the questions with a partner.

1. What question is the writer answering?

2. What is the writer's opinion? What ideas does he use to support his opinion?

B Read the question below and circle your answer. Then complete the notes. Research facts and experts' opinions to support your opinion.

> **Are ghosts real?** They might be. / They probably aren't.
> Fact(s) / Findings / Experts' opinions about this:
>
> 1.
>
> 2.

Does life exist on other planets? It might. **Scientists think that** there are billions of planets in the universe. Some of these planets may be similar to Earth. **In fact,** scientists found hundreds of planets like Earth last year. These planets might have water, and they might not be too hot or too cold. There could be simple life forms on them. Maybe one day we will solve this mystery.

C Use your ideas in **B** and the example in **A** to write a paragraph of your own.

D 🔁 Exchange papers with a partner.

1. Circle any mistakes in your partner's writing.

2. Answer question 2 in **A** about your partner's paragraph. Do you agree with your partner?

6 COMMUNICATION

A Look at the photos and read the notes about these unsolved mysteries. What do you think each thing is? Circle your answers.

The Yonaguni Monument

What: The Yonaguni Monument is a large underwater rock formation about 25 meters (82 feet) high in the Pacific Ocean, near Japan. The mysterious objects look like the pyramids in Egypt and the Americas.

a. an underwater city

b. a pyramid built by the Egyptians

c. nothing, just some rocks

d. your idea: _____

MARFA'S MYSTERY LIGHTS
VIEWING AREA
1 MILE

The Marfa Lights

What: The Marfa Lights are lights that appear suddenly in the night sky. Often, there are two or three of them. They are about the size of a basketball. Sometimes they fly close to people's houses. People first saw them in 1883 in the desert near the town of Marfa, Texas (US).

a. lights from a car or plane

b. some kind of strange weather

c. a UFO

d. your idea: _____

B 👥 Work in a small group. Discuss each of the possible answers to the question in **A**. Which is the most likely explanation?

> The Marfa Lights might be lights from a car or plane...

> No, they can't be because...

C 👥 Can you think of another unsolved mystery like the ones in **A** or on the Grammar page? Tell your group about the mystery. They will think of explanations for it.

1 STORYBOARD

A Susan, Maya, and Bruno work together. Look at the pictures and complete the conversations. For some blanks, more than one answer is possible.

B Practice the conversations with a group of three. Then change roles and practice again.

C Role-play. Introduce a friend to another friend. Invite both friends out to dinner.

2 SEE IT AND SAY IT

A  Below is a page from Anna Lopez's high school yearbook. She graduated in 2010. Read what her classmates wrote in her yearbook. How did Anna know each person? Discuss your ideas with a partner.

Sorry I didn't get to know you better, Anna. Good luck in college! Bobby

Hey, Anna! Best friends 4-ever! Rachel

Michael Evans   Bobby Leong   Anna Lopez   Rachel Williams

We're graduating, but you'll always be my girl, Anna. ~Michael

B Look below to see the people in **A** as they are today.

1. What are their relationships now?

2. Choose one of the pictures below. Make up a story about it. Answer these questions:
   - What happened to the people after high school?
   - How did they meet again?

3. Tell your partner the story of your picture.

Bobby and Anna

Rachel and Michael

3 LISTENING

A Look at the photos below. What words would you use to describe these things? Tell your partner.

B Four people are going to talk about their eating habits. Listen. Which food does each person like or eat a lot? Match a speaker (1, 2, 3, or 4) with the correct photo. **CD 1 Track 21**

C Read the sentences below. Then listen. Choose the correct answer for each sentence.
CD 1 Track 22

1. If you *get in shape*, you...
   a. gain weight.
   b. do things to be healthier.
   c. don't do much exercise.

2. If food tastes *bland*, it has...
   a. a strong taste.
   b. a lot of spices in it.
   c. no flavor.

3. If you *have a sweet tooth*, you...
   a. like sugary foods.
   b. can't eat sweets.
   c. are a good cook.

D Work with a partner. Follow the steps below. **CD 1 Track 21**

1. Write three more food items in the chart.

2. Listen again. Which person (1, 2, 3, or 4) probably eats the items on your list often?
   Check (✓) your answers.

Food or drink item	Person 1	Person 2	Person 3	Person 4
1. pizza				
2. a salad				
3. a candy bar				
4. _____				
5. _____				
6. _____				

3. Discuss your answers with a partner. Talk about the possibilities.

> I doubt that Person 1 eats pizza because...

E Which person (1, 2, 3, or 4) are you most like? Why? Tell your partner.

> I don't know. He might eat it because...

4 WONDERS OF THE WORLD

A 🔁 Use the adjectives in the box to ask and answer questions about these monuments with a partner.

beautiful	interesting	popular	strange
impressive	old	remote	tall

The Great Wall of China

The statues on Easter Island

The Eiffel Tower

The Roman Colosseum

Which monument is the oldest?

Well, the statues on Easter Island look old, but I think the Roman Colosseum is older.

5 I'M READING AN INTERESTING BOOK.

A Choose three words from the box. Write three sentences about yourself in your notebook. Use the simple present or the present continuous tense.

eat	know	like	own
read	study	work	

B 👥 Work in small groups. Read one of your sentences. Each person in your group asks a question about your sentence.

I always eat cereal for breakfast.

I'm reading an interesting book.

What kind of cereal do you eat?

Oh, really? What are you reading?

4 TRENDS

Look at the photo. Answer the questions.

1 A *trend* is a change toward something new or different. What is trendy (popular or fashionable) right now?

2 Do you ever do something (listen to certain music or buy a certain product) because a lot of people are doing it? Why or why not?

3 Do you follow fashion trends?

UNIT GOALS

1 Interpret numbers and talk about trends

2 Disagree with someone

3 Talk about fashion trends and your personal style

4 Give advice

A woman wears a stylish yellow hat in Ecuador.

There are over seven billion people in the world. What do you think the most "typical" person looks like?

1 **VIDEO** Are You Typical?

A Complete the sentences with information about yourself. How typical do you think you are? Discuss with a partner.

1. I am a(n) _60_-year-old _Brazilian_____ female / (male.)
   (e.g., Australian, French)

2. I am (right-handed) / left-handed, I (have) / don't have a cell phone, and (I have) / don't have a bank account.

B You are going to watch a video about the most typical person in the world. Read sentences 1–3 and try to guess the answers. Then watch and complete the sentences.

1. The most typical person is a(n) _20_-year-old _____chines_____ female / (male.)
2. The most typical person is (right-handed) / left-handed, (has) / doesn't have a cell phone, and has / (doesn't have) a bank account.
3. By 2030, the world's most typical person will come from ____China____.

C Discuss these questions with a partner.

1. Are you similar to the world's most typical person? Why or why not?
2. The video mentions a future change to the world's most typical person. What is it? What do you think is causing this change?

2 VOCABULARY

A 🔄 Look at the pie charts below. What do they show about student life in the United States? Tell a partner.

B 🔄 Read the sentences below each pair of pie charts. Circle the correct word to complete each sentence. Compare your answers with a partner's.

TRENDS IN AMERICAN STUDENT LIFE

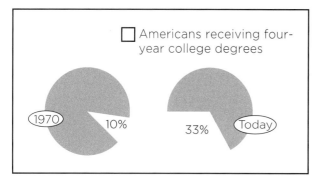
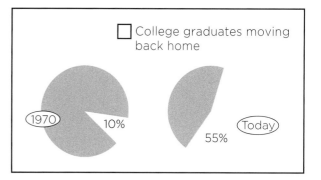

1. In 1970, about / exactly 10% of Americans received a four-year college degree.

2. Today that number is nearly / precisely 35%.

3. The number today is more than three times / four times as high.

4. The number of people with a college degree dropped / increased from 1970 to today.

5. In 1970, over / under 20% of college graduates moved back home to live with their parents.

6. Today, almost half / more than half of college graduates are moving back home.

7. There are more than four times / five times as many graduates moving home today.

8. The number of graduates moving back home rose / fell from 1970 to today.

C 🔄 Discuss the questions with a partner.

1. In your opinion, which trend(s) in **B** are positive? negative? Why?

2. Are these trends similar or different in your country? Explain.

3 LISTENING

A Infer information. Read about Alex below. What do you think the term *boomerang kid* means?

Alex is nearly 25 years old. He left home to go to college when he was 18 years old. He graduated from college over three years ago. About a year after graduation, he moved back home to live with his parents. Alex is known as a "boomerang kid."

B 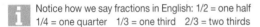 **Make predictions.** Look at the chart. Read the information about Alex's life before, his life now, and his hopes for the future. What do you think he is going to say about his life? Tell a partner.

> ℹ️ Notice how we say fractions in English: 1/2 = one half
> 1/4 = one quarter   1/3 = one third   2/3 = two thirds

Nearly 50% of college graduates move back home at some point.

	Before	**Now**	**In the future**
Living situation	lived in an _____	lives at _____	going to find a _____
Rent	more than _____ a month	_____	going to _____ the rent
Money	didn't have _____ of money	saves _____ of his salary	
Work	couldn't find _____	works _____	wants to find a _____ job

C 🔊 **Check predictions.** Listen to Alex talk about his life. As you listen, complete the chart in **B**.
CD 1 Track 23

D 🔊 **Listen for details.** Listen. Complete the paragraph. **CD 1 Track 24**

My mother told me not to give up. But it's not so _____. When my mom was _____, she graduated from college and _____ a job pretty quickly. Now more people go to college, and there is more competition for _____. It's a lot _____.

E 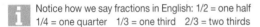 Read the paragraph in **D**. Then discuss the questions below with a partner.

1. Do you think it's harder for college graduates now? Why or why not?
2. When do children typically move out of their parents' home in your country? Do they ever move back home? If so, why?

4 SPEAKING

A 🔊 🔁 Listen to the conversation. Then answer the questions with a partner. **CD 1 Track 25**

1. What are Carla and her dad fighting about?
2. Who do you agree with, Carla or her dad?

CARLA: Dad, can I talk to you for a minute?

DAD: Sure, what's up?

CARLA: Well, my friend Marta is going to see a concert tomorrow night, and she invited me to go.

DAD: Tomorrow night? But tomorrow's Tuesday. Sorry, Carla, but no.

CARLA: Dad! You *never* let me do anything.

DAD: That's not true, Carla. You do lots of things. But the concert ends late, and you have school on Wednesday.

CARLA: I know what you're saying, Dad, but it's just one night. And all of my friends are going.

DAD: Sorry, Carla, but the answer is still no.

CARLA: Oh, Dad, you're so unfair!

B 🔁 Practice the conversation with a partner.

SPEAKING STRATEGY

C 🔁 Work with a partner. One person is the parent. The other person is the son or daughter.

1. Choose a situation from the box below. Think of reasons for and against it.
2. Create a new conversation similar to the one in **A**. Include at least two Useful Expressions.

D 🔾 Get together with another pair.

- **Pair 1:** Perform your conversation for another pair.
- **Pair 2:** Listen. Who do you agree with—the parent or child? Why?

E 🔾 Switch roles and do **D** again.

Useful Expressions	
Disagreeing	Disagreeing more strongly
I know what you're saying, but… I see what you mean, but… Yes, (that may be true), but… I'm not so sure about that.	I'm afraid I disagree. Sorry, but I disagree. That's (just) not true. I totally / completely disagree.
Speaking tip	
You can soften your disagreement by first saying that you understand the other person's point. *I see what you mean, but I still don't think it's a good idea.*	

Parents: Your son or daughter wants to…

- go on a date.
- visit another country by himself or herself.
- get a part-time job.
- your own idea: _____

5 GRAMMAR

A Turn to page 199. Complete the exercises. Then do **B–D** below.

Quantity Expressions				
Quantity	*of*	**Determiner**	**Plural count noun**	
All **Most** **A lot** **Half** **Some** **None**	of	my	friends	live at home.
		Pronoun		
		them		

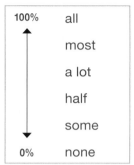

100%	all
	most
	a lot
	half
	some
0%	none

B 🔊 **Pronunciation: Unstressed *of*.** Practice saying the three sentences below. Then listen and repeat. Notice the pronunciation of the word *of* in each one. **CD 1 Track 26**

1. A lot of college graduates move back home.
2. Most of my friends live at home.
3. Some of them have part-time jobs.

Word Bank
a couple = two

C Read the information about six families from around the world. Then write *all*, *most*, *a lot*, *some*, *a couple*, or *none* in the blanks below.

	The SHAW family	The IKEDA family	The OLIVEIRA family	The CHOI family	The VEGA family	The KUMAR family
Hometown	Chicago	Tokyo	São Paulo	Seoul	Mexico City	New Delhi
Language	English	Japanese	Portuguese	Korean	Spanish	English
Housing	house	apartment	apartment	apartment	house	apartment
Transportation	car	subway	bus	car	car	bus
Wife works at...	restaurant	office	hotel	office	office	office
Children	no	yes	yes	yes	yes	yes

1. _____ of the families live in big cities.
2. _____ of the families speak English.
3. _____ of them speak French.
4. _____ of the families live in apartments.
5. _____ of them own cars.
6. _____ of the wives work.
7. _____ of them work in an office.
8. _____ of the families have children.

D 🔄 Tell your partner about the families you know using *all (of)*, *most (of)*, *a lot (of)*, *half (of)*, *some (of)*, *a couple (of)*, or *none (of)*. Use the list below.

have children   speak a little English   live in the city

live in a house / apartment   own a car   have a mother who works

6 COMMUNICATION

A Read the situations below. For each one, choose the answer you agree with or write your own idea.

Luis wants to go to design school, but his father wants him to go to City University. Luis doesn't want to go there, but if he doesn't, his father will not pay for school. What should Luis do?

a. Go to City University like his father wants.
b. Start at City University and then later transfer (move) to another school.
c. Get a job, save his money, and pay for his own education.
d. Your idea: _____

Yukiko's 16-year-old brother hangs out with some bad people. He isn't going to class, and he is fighting at school. Yukiko is worried. What should she do?

a. Wait a little longer. Maybe things will change.
b. Talk to her brother. Tell him her feelings.
c. Tell her parents about her brother.
d. Your idea: _____

Josh is dating Holly. Josh loves her, but his parents don't like her. This weekend is Josh's birthday. His parents are having a party, and they have invited all his friends—except Holly. What should Josh do?

a. Talk to his parents and tell them to invite Holly.
b. Just bring Holly to the party.
c. Skip the party and spend the day with Holly.
d. Your idea: _____

B 👥 Get into a small group. Talk about your opinions in **A**. Explain the reasons for your choices.

> I think Luis should
> go to City University.

C 👥 Look back at each situation in **A**. How many people in your group agreed with answers a–c? How many came up with their own answers? Compare your results with another group.

> Most of our group members think
> Luis should go to City University.

> Really? Most of us think he should
> go to design school.

Fashion Flashback

What styles were in (popular) a decade ago?

1 VOCABULARY

A 🔄 Work with a partner. Look at the photos and read the question. Then match the words (a–e) below with the clothing items in the photos.

a. **ripped** jeans

b. **baggy** shorts

c. **pointy** shoes

d. an **oversized** shirt

e. **skinny (fitted)** jeans

B 🔄 Answer the questions with a partner.

1. Are the styles above still in?

2. Which words in the box do you know? Which are new?

3. Which words in the box describe the styles in the photos? Which describe your look?

Word Bank
Describing your look (style)
casual / comfortable ↔ formal / conservative
colorful
dramatic / flashy ↔ plain / simple
elegant
retro / vintage
stylish
sporty
unique / unusual ↔ common / ordinary

2 LISTENING

  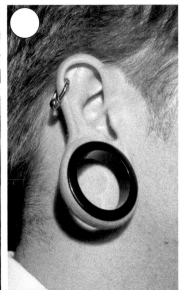 

A 🔄 **Use background knowledge.** Look at the photos and answer the questions with a partner.

1. What are the people in the photos wearing?

2. What adjectives from page 56 describe each person's look?

Word Bank

dress code = the rules about the clothes a person can wear in a place (at work, at school)

B 🔊 **Listen for gist.** Listen. You will hear three different conversations. What are the people talking about? Number the photos (1, 2, or 3). One photo is extra. **CD 1 Track 27**

C 🔊 **Listen for a speaker's opinion.** Read the sentences below. Then listen again. Circle the correct word and write one word in each blank. **CD 1 Track 27**

Photo 1

1. The woman likes / ~~dislikes~~ the ear piercings because they're too _____big_____.

2. The man ~~likes~~ / dislikes the style. He says it's a _____cool_____ look.

Photo 2

3. The man's office dress code is mostly "business _____casual_____."

4. The man ~~likes~~ / dislikes his office dress code. It's more _____comfortable_____ than the one at his last job.

Photo 3

5. The girl says her brother's look is very _____retro_____.

6. The girl likes / ~~dislikes~~ this style because it's _____fun_____.

D 🔄 Answer the questions with a partner.

1. Do you like the styles in the photos? Why or why not?

2. Does your school or workplace have a dress code? Explain.

3 READING

A 🔄 **Make predictions.** Read the ad below. Then answer the questions with a partner.

1. What do you think a trendspotter does?
2. Who would hire a trendspotter?

> Are you between the ages of 15 and 22? Do you like fashion and music? Do you know what's hip?
>
> You could be a **trendspotter**!
> • Try new products!
> • Participate in surveys!
> • Receive free samples!

B **Check predictions; Read for gist.** Brooke is 18 years old. She works as a trendspotter. What does she do? Read her posts and check your answers in **A**.

C **Sentence insertion.** Write each sentence below in the correct place in the reading. One sentence is extra.

Yesterday, they were here in the studio.

I can't wait for our next meeting!

Then she gave us a tour of the studio.

There were about ten of us.

D 🔄 **Understand paraphrases.** Check (✓) the sentence(s) Brooke would say about being a trendspotter. Explain your answers to a partner.

1. _____ It's kind of boring.
2. _____ You can make good money.
3. _____ You get free things.
4. _____ You work with famous people.
5. _____ People ask your opinion about lots of things.

E 🔄 Answer the questions with a partner.

1. Why do you think companies use trendspotters? Do you think it's a good idea?
2. Would you like to be a trendspotter? Why or why not?

TRENDSPOTTING

Part-time Job

Today I started my new part-time job as a trendspotter. I was nervous and didn't know what to expect. Well, guess what? It was a lot of fun! I'm telling all of my friends, "You should think about becoming a trendspotter, too!"

This morning, we had to report to a recording studio[1] by 10 AM. The "Trends Coordinator," Mandy, explained the schedule. _____. That was really cool!

Next we sat around a big table in a room. _____. Mandy gave each person three cards. One card said "Yes—All the way!" Another said, "It's OK." The third one said, "No way!" We listened to about ten different songs. After each song, we had to hold up a card. They played some hip-hop, rock, heavy metal, and dance music. The heavy metal was "No way!" for me!

Gifted

Do you know the rock group Gifted? They're really popular right now. _____. Too bad we missed them. Anyway, they have a new album coming out soon. We saw six different album covers. (I guess they are trying to choose one.) This time, we didn't have any cards. Instead, we just talked about the covers we liked. Mandy asked us questions: "Which ones do you like?" and "Why do you like them?"

We finished at 12:30. We meet again next week at a boutique[2] downtown. We will look at some new fashions. Each week we go to a different location. Oh, and we also received a gift card for our work. This "job" doesn't pay, but we get free stuff!

That's all for now!

[1]Musicians make music in a *recording studio*.
[2]A *boutique* is a small store.

4 GRAMMAR

A Turn to page 200. Complete the exercise. Then do **B** and **C** below.

Giving Advice with *could, should, ought to,* and *had better*	
You **could** wear a dress to the party. You **could** wear the blue dress or the black one.	Use *could* to make a suggestion or give advice. It is often used to offer two or more choices.
You **should / ought to** wear a formal suit to the job interview. You **shouldn't** wear jeans. They're too casual.	Use *should* or *ought to* to give advice. Both are stronger than *could*.
You'**d better** wear a coat. It's going to rain. We'**d better not** drive to the concert. It will be hard to park.	Use *had better (not)* to give strong advice.

B 🔁 Look at the list and think of three pieces of advice to give your partner.

Student A: You are going to an informal birthday party at an American friend's home.

Student B: You are going to a formal dinner party at the British consulate.

arrive a little late	wear a suit or a nice dress	wear ripped jeans
bring food	bring a friend who wasn't invited	wear something elegant
wear casual clothes	bring flowers or a small gift to the host	wear unique clothes

C 🔁 Work with a partner. Tell your partner your plans. He or she will give you some advice and explain it.

> I'm going to a birthday party at an American friend's home. Should I bring something?

> Yeah, you could bring..., but you shouldn't...

5 WRITING

A 🔁 Read the post from Sad Sam. What is his problem? Tell a partner.

B Now write a response to Sam. Give him some advice.

C 🔁 Exchange papers with a partner.

1. Correct any mistakes in your partner's writing.

2. Do you agree with your partner's advice? Why or why not?

Ask Susie Style

Dear Susie Style,

I need your help! I can't get a job. Everywhere I go, I get the same answer: "No!" Is my appearance the problem? Here is a picture of me. What do you think? What should I do?

Sad Sam

6 COMMUNICATION

A Ask your partner the questions. Check (✓) your partner's answers.

How often do you...	often	sometimes	never
1. wear "the same old thing"?	☐	☐	☐
2. buy something because it's cheap?	☐	☐	☐
3. wear something comfortable but mismatched?	☐	☐	☐
4. wear something until it's worn out?	☐	☐	☐
5. leave the house without looking in the mirror?	☐	☐	☐
6. read fashion magazines about new trends?	☐	☐	☐
7. change your hairstyle?	☐	☐	☐
8. shop for new clothes or shoes?	☐	☐	☐

B Calculate your partner's score. Use the table.

	For questions 1–5	For questions 6–8
often	score 2 points	score 0 points
sometimes	score 1 point	score 1 point
never	score 0 points	score 2 points

Word Bank

If something is *worn out*, it is old and unusable.

If you *get a makeover*, you do things to improve your look.

C Read the appropriate advice to your partner. What does your partner think of the advice?

0–3 points: You know what's "in," and you're very stylish. Keep up the great work!	**4–7 points:** You have a good sense of style, but you could change a few things or just try to do something new every week.	**8–12 points:** Your look might be a little plain. You could change something about your clothing or hairstyle. You should also try to go out more and see what's happening.	**13–16 points:** You scored a lot of points. You'd better think about getting a complete makeover!

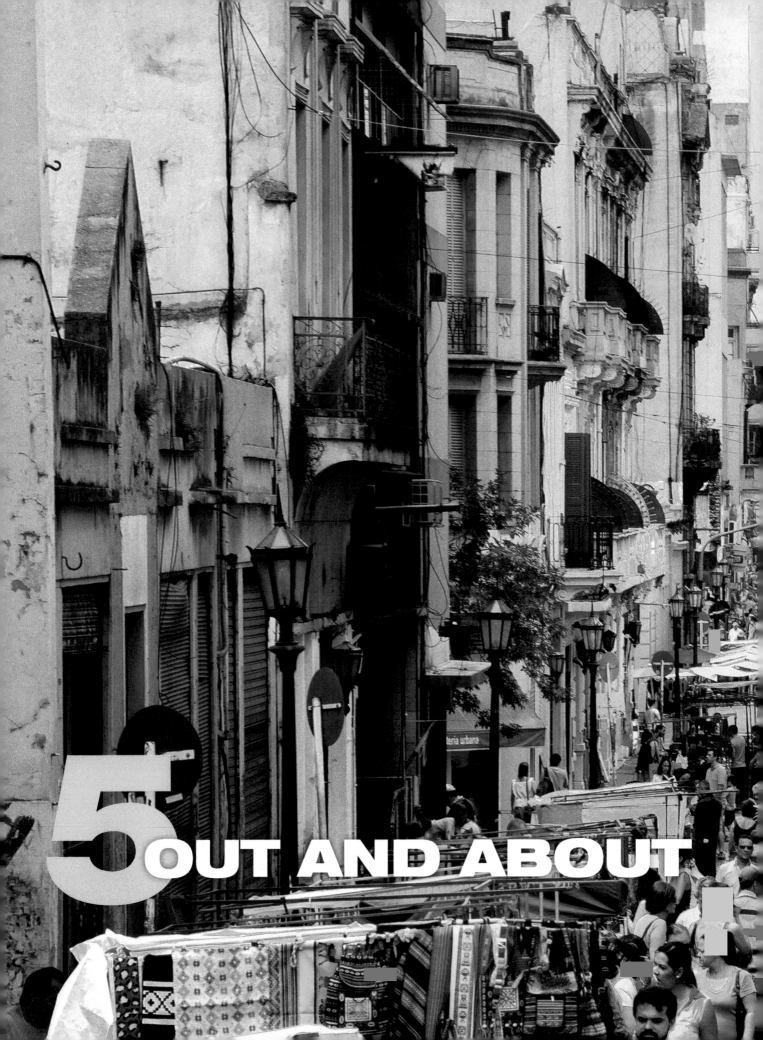

5 OUT AND ABOUT

Look at the photo. Answer the questions.

1 Do you live in a city like this?

2 Where do you think these people are going?

3 What is a popular neighborhood in your city?

UNIT GOALS

1 Describe household chores

2 Make and reschedule appointments

3 Make and respond to requests

4 Describe your neighborhood

**San Telmo Market in
Buenos Aires, Argentina**

Amsterdam has around 1,500 bridges and more than 100 kilometers (62 miles) of canals.

1 **VIDEO** Bicycle Anecdotes from Amsterdam

A You are going to watch a video about *getting around* (traveling around) Amsterdam. Answer the questions with a partner.

1. What do you know about the city?
2. There are two major ways to get around the city. What do you think they are?

B Watch the video and answer the questions. Circle T for *True* and F for *False*.

1. In the inner canal area, both bikes and cars go fast.		T	F
2. On the main roads, there are off-street bike paths.		T	F
3. The bike system is mainly for students.		T	F
4. There are many more cars than bikes on the busiest streets.		T	F

C Look at your answers in **B**. What do you think of Amsterdam's "bike culture"? Do many people ride bikes in your country? Why or why not? Tell a partner.

2 VOCABULARY

A Work with a partner. Match the sentence parts.

1. You **do the dishes**…
2. You **do laundry**…
3. You **drop off** your younger brother or sister…
4. You **go grocery shopping**…
5. You **make a reservation**…
6. You **make** a doctor's **appointment**…
7. You **make dinner**…
8. You **pick up** your younger brother or sister…
9. You **sweep**… to remove dust and dirt.
10. You **vacuum**… to remove dust and dirt.

a. at school in the morning.
b. for dinner at a restaurant.
c. after you eat.
d. the floors
e. in the evening.
f. when you feel sick.
g. when your clothes are dirty.
h. the rugs
i. when you have no food in the house.
j. after school.

B Which activity do you have to do soon? Complete the sentence. Then tell a partner.

I have to _____.

> I have to pick up some food at the market tonight. I'm having a dinner party tomorrow!

C Complete the questions with the verbs from **A**. Use the correct form of the verb.

1. Do you ever _____ the dishes?
2. When was the last time you _____ dinner for yourself? What did you eat?
3. Who usually _____ the laundry in your house?
4. How often do you _____ the floors or _____ the rugs in your bedroom?
5. When was the last time you _____ an appointment for yourself? Who did you see?
6. When you _____ grocery shopping, what's something you always buy?
7. Have you ever _____ a reservation for dinner? Where did you go?
8. Do you ever _____ off or _____ up someone at school?

D Take turns asking and answering the questions in **C** with a partner. Then discuss: How many of your chores and errands can you do in your neighborhood?

A market in Granada, Spain

3 LISTENING

A 🔊 **Listen for gist.** Read the sentences. Then listen to four different phone calls. Circle the correct words to complete each sentence. **CD 1 Track 29**

1. The woman is calling to make / change a hotel / restaurant reservation.

2. The man wants to drop off / pick up his pants / shirts at the dry cleaner.

3. The man is calling to make / change a doctor's / dentist appointment.

4. The girl needs a ride to school / the doctor's office.

B 🔊 **Identify a response.** What would the speaker say next in each conversation? Listen again and circle your answers. Some items have two correct answers. **CD 1 Track 29**

1. a. Sorry, but the only other time available is 9:00 PM.
   b. Yes, we can add two more people to the reservation.
   c. Sure, no problem. How is 7:30 for you?

2. a. No, tomorrow's better.
   b. Perfect. I'll see you at 5:00.
   c. Okay, I can drop them off later.

3. a. Ten works for me. See you then.
   b. Great. See you tomorrow afternoon.
   c. That doesn't work for me. Do you have anything later?

4. a. OK, I'll see you at school later.
   b. Sure. I'll pick you up in fifteen minutes.
   c. Yes, it is.

C 🔄 With a partner, complete each conversation in **B** by adding one more sentence to one of the correct answer choices. Then role-play one of your conversations.

> We want to change our reservation.

> Sure, no problem. How is 7:30 for you?

> Great. See you then.

D 🔊 **Pronunciation: Reduced forms of *could you* and *would you*.** Listen. Notice the reduced pronunciation of *could you* and *would you* in each question. Then repeat the questions. **CD 1 Track 30**

1. Could you open the window, please?
2. Could you drop me off at school?
3. Would you mind making dinner tonight?
4. Would you pick up your socks from the floor?

E 🔊 **Pronunciation: Reduced forms of *could you* and *would you*.** Listen to the questions. Circle the words you hear. **CD 1 Track 31**

1. Could you / Would you turn down the TV, please?
2. Could you / Would you make a dinner reservation for four people?
3. Could you / Would you spell your last name, please?
4. Could you / Would you take notes for me in class today?

F 🔄 With a partner, say the questions in **D** and **E** with the reduced forms of *could you* and *would you*.

4 SPEAKING

A 🔊 🔁 Listen to the conversation. Then answer the questions with a partner. **CD 1 Track 32**

1. Why is Minh calling the language center?
2. When is he planning to go there?

MARTINA: Hello, ISS Language Center. This is Martina.

MINH: Yeah, hi. I'm in a TOEFL class that starts next week. I'd like to make an appointment to see the student counselor first.

MARTINA: Sure. I can help you with that. Let's see, can you come in tomorrow at 10:30?

MINH: No, that time isn't good for me. Do you have anything later in the day?

MARTINA: Let me check. OK, how's 4:15?

MINH: That's perfect.

MARTINA: Great. Now, I just need to get your name.

MINH: It's Minh Nguyen.

MARTINA: Could you spell your last name for me, please?

MINH: Sure, it's N-G-U-Y-E-N.

B 🔁 Practice the conversation with a partner.

SPEAKING STRATEGY

Useful Expressions: Making Appointments
Explaining why you're calling

I'm calling to… / I'd like to…
       make an appointment with a counselor / Dr. Smith / the dentist.
       make a dentist / doctor's / hair appointment.
       reschedule my appointment / our meeting.

Scheduling the time
Can you come in / Could we meet / How's tomorrow at 2:00?   That's perfect. / That works for me.   No, that (time / day) doesn't work for me.

C 🔁 With a partner, create a new conversation like the one in **A**. Use the situation below and at least two Useful Expressions.

Student A: You want to make an appointment to get a haircut on Thursday afternoon.

Student B: You work at a hair salon. On Thursday, you are free at 11:30 AM. You also have some afternoon appointments on the weekend.

D 🔁 Switch roles and repeat with the situation below.

Student A: You and your classmate usually meet on Tuesday to practice English. You want to reschedule for Wednesday at 1:00, but you can also meet on Friday.

Student B: You can only meet on Thursday or Friday after 1:00.

5 GRAMMAR

A Turn to page 201. Complete the exercises. Then do **B–D** below.

Requests with Modal Verbs and *mind*			
Making requests			**Responding to requests**
Can / Will you **Could / Would** you	help	me, please?	Sure, no problem. / I'd be glad to. / Of course. / Sure thing. I'm sorry, / I'd like to, but I can't.
Would you **mind**	helping		No, not at all. / No, I'd be glad to. I'm sorry, / I'd like to, but I can't.

B 🔁 Work with a partner. Take 16 small pieces of paper. On eight, write the numbers from 1 to 8. Shuffle these and put them face down on the desk. Then on four pieces of paper, write the word *Yes*. On the other four, write *No.* Shuffle these and put them face down in a different pile.

C 🔁 You and your partner are college roommates. Read the list of eight requests in the box. Read the example. Then follow the instructions below.

1. **Student A:** Turn over a number (1–8). Ask your roommate to do this activity from the list. Explain why you need the favor.

2. **Student B:** Turn over a *Yes / No* paper and respond in the correct way.

3. Change roles and repeat steps 1 and 2. Take turns and continue until you do all eight.

> 1. make dinner tonight
> 2. take notes for me in class tomorrow
> 3. pick up my clothes at the dry cleaner
> 4. drop me off at the mall
> 5. loan me some money for lunch
> 6. be a little quieter after 11:00 PM
> 7. do my laundry
> 8. introduce me to your cute friend

A: Jin, could you do me a favor? Would you mind taking notes for me in class tomorrow? I have a dentist appointment.

B: No, not all.

A: Great, thanks!

A: Jin, can you take notes for me in class tomorrow? I have a dentist appointment.

B: Sorry, but I won't be in class tomorrow either.

A: No problem. I'll ask someone else.

D Think about the requests you made in **C**. For any of them, did you use *Would you mind…*? Why?

6 COMMUNICATION

A Look at the photo and read the information. What would you pay a *benriya* to do for you? Think of one idea.

B  Work with a partner and create your own benriya service. Answer the questions.

- What services do you offer (doing housework, running errands, fixing things, etc.)?

- How much do you charge for each service?

- What is your company's name, and when do you work?

C Get together with a new partner. Sit back-to-back. Do the following. Then switch roles.

- Call your new partner's benriya service.

- Use your idea from **A**. Explain what you want the service to do for you.

- Ask what your partner's service charges.

- Make an appointment with the service.

> A: Hello, Handy Helpers Service. How can I help you?
>
> B: Hi. I'd like some information about your service.
>
> A: Sure, what exactly do you need us to do?
>
> B: I want to break up with my boyfriend.
>
> A: No problem! We can do that for you.
>
> B: Great. Could you tell me how much you charge, please?

D Repeat **C** with three other partners. Of the four benriya services you talked to, which is the best? Tell the class.

Many cities, like Rio de Janeiro in Brazil, are becoming more pedestrian and bicycle friendly.

1 VOCABULARY

A 🔖 Look at the photo and, with a partner, point to these things: *the sidewalk*, *the pedestrians*, *the bike lane*.

B 🔖 Read the information below. Then look at the photo. Is this a walkable area? Why or why not? Tell a partner.

Is your neighborhood **walkable**? In a walkable neighborhood:

1. It's easy to **get around on foot** because **sidewalks** are in good condition.

2. It's safe for **pedestrians** (people walking) to cross the street. Drivers are careful. There isn't a lot of **traffic**.

3. There are bike **lanes** in the street so cyclists can ride safely.

4. It's easy to **get to** other parts of the city by bus or by subway.

Word Bank
get around = to go from one place to another place
get to (a place) = to travel to a place

C 🔖 Is your neighborhood walkable? Tell your partner. Explain with reasons 1–4 in **B**.

> It isn't safe for pedestrians to cross the street in my neighborhood. Drivers are crazy!

D 🔄 Ask your partner the questions. Answer in two ways: with *by / on* and with a verb. Use the chart to help you.

1. How do you get around your neighborhood?

   by / on _____

   I usually _____.

2. How do you get to school or work?

   by / on _____

   I usually _____.

2 LISTENING

A 🔄 Where is the neighborhood in the photo? What do you think it's like? Tell a partner.

B 🔊 **Listen for the main idea.** Read the sentences. Then listen and circle the best answer. **CD 1 Track 33**

Two international students in Seoul are talking. They are mainly discussing _____ Hongdae.

a. the best way to get to   c. the problems with

b. a popular street in

C 🔊 **Listen for details.** Read the sentences. Then listen again. Circle the correct answer. **CD 1 Track 33**

The woman says…

1. the area is / isn't easy to get to by bike.

2. it's best to go to Hongdae by car / on public transportation.

3. Hongdae is / isn't easy to get around on foot.

4. it's faster to go to Hongdae by bus / subway.

D 🔊 **Identify key details.** What information helped you choose your answers in **C**? Listen again and write the words or numbers you hear. **CD 1 Track 33**

1. There's a lot of _____, and there aren't many _____ for cyclists.

2. It's better to take the _____ and then get around Hongdae _____.

3. Hongdae is a very _____ area.

4. If you take the _____, it's about _____ minutes. By _____, it's only _____.

E 🔄 Is there an area like Hongdae in your city? What's it like? How can you get there? Tell a partner.

Describing Ways of Going Places		
by / on + transportation		verbs
by	bike	ride my bike
	bus / subway	take the bus / subway
	car	drive
	taxi	take a taxi
	train	take / catch the train
on	foot	walk

Notice the two ways to say the same thing:
1. I usually get around my neighborhood *on foot*.
2. I usually *walk*.

Hongdae is a trendy area in Seoul, South Korea.

3 READING

I LOVE MY NEIGHBORHOOD

Two students write about their neighborhoods and why each is special.

A 🔄 **Skim for the main idea.** Read the title and the sentence below it. Then look quickly at the photos and the passage. What is this article mainly about? Where are the neighborhoods? Tell a partner.

B 🔄 **Read for details.** Work with a partner. Each person should choose one neighborhood, read about it, and then answer the questions below.

1. What is the neighborhood's name?

2. Is it a busy or quiet neighborhood?

3. Is it a walkable neighborhood?

4. What are some special things about the neighborhood?

C 🔄 Ask your partner the questions in **B** about the neighborhood he or she chose. Take notes. Then read about your partner's neighborhood to check his or her answers.

D **Scan for information.** What does each number describe? Look quickly through the reading to find the answers.

1. 5.4   <u>The size of Inwood</u>

2. 20   _____

3. 200   _____

4. 859   _____

5. 1,200   _____

6. 9,000   _____

7. 10,000   _____

E 🔄 Answer the questions with a partner.

1. How are the two neighborhoods similar to or different from yours?

2. Which one would you like to visit? Why?

WORLD LINK

Go online to learn one more thing about Inwood or Fes el Bali. Share it with the class.

I live in Fes el Bali, a neighborhood in the city of Fes in Morocco. My neighborhood is over 1,200 years old, and it's a very busy place. In fact, there are almost 10,000 businesses here. We've also got one of the oldest universities in the world. It opened in the year 859.

Fes el Bali is surrounded by a high wall with gates. You can drive inside the main gate, but then you can only travel through the streets on foot, by bicycle,… or donkey! In fact, Fes el Bali is one of the largest car-free pedestrian areas in the world. And speaking of the streets, there are over 9,000 of them. It's easy to get around my neighborhood, but be careful: the streets aren't straight. They're very long and winding, and it's easy to get lost! If you're ever in Morocco, be sure to spend some time in my neighborhood: Fes el Bali. It's a place you'll never forget!

When people hear the word "Manhattan," many think of tall buildings, theaters, and crowded streets. My neighborhood—Inwood—is also in Manhattan, but it's very different from the rest of New York City. For example, this neighborhood has a forest. Many of its trees are hundreds of years old, and there are lots of small animals and wild birds. You can go hiking in some parts of the forest and get lost!

Many buildings in this neighborhood are old, too. For example, there's a farmhouse near my home. It's over 200 years old. Today it's a museum.

Inwood is about 5.4 square kilometers (2 square miles), so it's easy to get around on foot or by bike. And unlike the rest of New York City, Inwood is a pretty quiet place. But it's still very easy to get to the other parts of the city. You can take the subway and in 20 minutes, you're in downtown Manhattan. If you're ever in New York City, come and visit Inwood and see a part of Manhattan you didn't know existed. You'll be glad you did!

4 GRAMMAR

A Turn to page 202. Complete the exercises. Then do **B** and **C** below.

Modifiers *really* / *very* and *pretty*			
	Adverb	**Adjective**	
It's	**really / very** **pretty**	far	from here.
	Adverb	**Adjective + noun**	
It's a	**really / very** **pretty**	long walk	from here.

B Make the sentences true for you. Then add *very*, *really*, or *pretty* to each sentence.

1. I have a _____ busy / relaxed schedule.

2. I live in a _____ noisy / quiet neighborhood.

3. It's _____ easy / hard to get around my neighborhood on foot.

4. My neighborhood is _____ clean / dirty.

5. It's _____ easy / hard to get a taxi in my neighborhood.

6. My neighbors are _____ friendly / reserved people.

> I have a very busy
> schedule. I go to school
> Monday to Friday.
> I work, too.

C 🔄 Take turns telling a partner your sentences in **B**. Explain each one.

5 WRITING

A 🔄 Read the paragraph. Then answer the questions with a partner.

1. Where does the writer live?

2. Does he like his neighborhood? What three reasons does he give?

I live in Madrid in a neighborhood called Pacifico. I like living here for three reasons. **First**, it's convenient. It's really easy to get around by subway or bus. I can go anywhere in the city, and I don't need a car. It is **also** a very walkable neighborhood. There are a lot of stores and restaurants. I can walk to the supermarket or my favorite cafe in five minutes. There's a big park in my neighborhood, too. It's a great place to ride your bike. **And finally**, Pacifico is a pretty quiet neighborhood. I live on a busy street. It's noisy during the day, but at night it's not. I like that.

B Complete an outline about your neighborhood. Use a different adjective in each reason. Explain each reason with an extra sentence or two.

> I live in a neighborhood in _____ called _____.
> I like / don't like living here for three reasons.
>
> 1. It's _____. _____.
> 2. It's _____. _____.
> 3. It's _____. _____.

C Use your outline in **B** and the example in **A** to help you write a paragraph of your own. Use *very*, *really*, or *pretty* at least twice in your paragraph.

D 🔄 Exchange papers with a partner.

1. Circle any mistakes in your partner's writing.
2. Answer the questions in **A** about your partner's neighborhood.
3. Would you like to live in your partner's neighborhood? Why or why not? Tell your partner.

6 COMMUNICATION

A 🔄 With a partner, think of a problem in a neighborhood in your city. Use the ideas below. Then think of at least one solution to the problem. Explain why it's a good idea.

Problem: In (name of neighborhood) _____…

- it's difficult for pedestrians to cross the streets safely.
- the sidewalks are really dirty.
- public transportation is terrible. It's hard to get to other parts of the city.
- it's dangerous to walk alone at night.
- there are no fun things to do.
- other: _____

Our solution: _____

Why it's a good idea: _____

B 👥 Get together with another pair. Present your problem and explain your solution(s). The other pair will listen, answer the question below, and explain their opinion. Then switch roles and repeat.

What do you think of their idea?

- I really like the idea because…
- The idea is pretty good, but…
- Sorry, but I don't think the idea will work because…

> The sidewalks in this neighborhood are really dirty. Our solution is to…

C 👥 Repeat **B** with a different pair.

6 GOALS

People work together at Google's European headquarters in Dublin, Ireland.

Look at the photo. Answer the questions.

1 What are some of the most well-known companies in your country?

2 Do you know anyone who works at these places?

3 Would you want to work at a place like the one in the photo?

UNIT GOALS

1 Describe how to apply to a school

2 Respond to bad news and offer to help

3 Talk about educational and work goals

4 Make predictions about the future

A *job fair* (also, *career fair*) is an event where job hunters can meet many possible employers in one place.

1 **VIDEO** Young Entrepreneurs

A Read the statistic from the video. What do you think the video is going to be about? Tell a partner.

Only 1 in 4 college graduates will graduate with a job.

B There are four people in the video. Read the items in the chart. Then watch the video. Check (✓) the answers.

	Jason Zima	John Campbell	Scott Gerber	Christy Tyler
is a senior at Babson College				
feels discouraged				
got a job while still in school				
majored in business	✓			
opened a shoe store				
started a photography business				
started several businesses				
teaches business classes				
went to a job fair	✓			

C Discuss the questions with a partner.

1. Look at your answers in **B**. Who do you think is going to be most successful? Why?

2. Are there job fairs in your country?

3. How do new college graduates find jobs? How hard is it?

2 VOCABULARY

A Read the instructions for applying to college in the United States. Finish writing the incomplete words. Use the correct form of the words in the Word Bank.

- Look at different colleges' websites. (1.) _Con_____ these questions: Where is the school located? Does it offer your major? How big are the class sizes?

- Make a list of all the colleges that interest you.

- Top schools receive thousands of (2.) _app_____. There is a lot of (3.) _com_____ for few openings. Be realistic in your goals.

- Visit some of the schools on your list. Talk to students at the school. How do they like it?

- (4.) _Ob_____ some classes at the school. Are the classes interesting?

- Ask your high school teachers to write letters of (5.) _rec_____ for you.

- (6.) _De_____ which schools to (7.) _app_____ to. Your (8.) _app_____ should be sent no later than January.

- Most schools will give you their (9.) _de_____ by April. You choose your school in May and start in August or September.

  Good luck!

B ⟳ Review the steps in **A** with a partner. How is applying to college different in your country? How is it similar?

> **Usage notes**
> apply **to** a school, decide **to do** something, consider **doing** something, recommend **that** someone do something

C ⚬ Read the message Kento posted on an online forum. What is Kento's problem? What advice would you give him? Discuss in small groups.

I'm trying to choose a college. My parents want me to apply to Tokyo University. It's one of the best colleges in Japan, and it's very competitive. I'm not even sure I want to go to college right now. I need some advice because I can't decide what to do!

—Kento

Tokyo University

Kento should consider waiting a year. He doesn't have to apply to college right now.

But what about his parents' feelings? I recommend that he...

3 LISTENING

A You're going to hear an interview about a special school. How do you think Stratton Mountain School is special? Look at the profile below and guess the answers.

B 🔊 **Listen for details.** A student is going to talk about the school below. Listen and complete the profile. **CD 1 Track 35**

STRATTON MOUNTAIN SCHOOL

Stratton Mountain School is a _____-year _____ school for students between _____ and _____ years old.

Where: Vermont, US

Students: Most are _____ or snowboarders. After graduation, some compete in the Winter _____.

A typical day at Stratton:

7:00 AM: _____

8:00 AM to _____:
Students are in _____.

12:30 to 5:00 PM:
Students have _____.

C 🔄 **Summarize.** Review the profile in **B**. Then cover your notes and answer the questions about Stratton with a partner.

1. Who goes to Stratton?   2. Why do they go there?   3. What is a typical day like?

D 🔊 Read the sentences below. Then listen. Choose the correct answer for each one.
CD 1 Track 36

1. A *coed* school admits…	2. A *dorm* is where students…	3. A school's *alumni* are…
a. boys only.	a. live.	a. graduates of the school.
b. girls only.	b. train.	b. students now at the school.
c. both boys and girls.	c. study.	c. teachers at the school.

E 🔄 Do you think Stratton is an interesting school? Why or why not? Discuss with a partner.

4 SPEAKING

A 🔊 🔁 Listen to the conversation. Then answer the questions with a partner. **CD 1 Track 37**

1. Tom is unhappy about something. What?
2. How does Hans respond to Tom's bad news? Underline Hans's responses.
3. Do you think Hans is a good friend? Why or why not?

HANS: Hey, Tom. How's it going with the college applications?

TOM: Not so well. I didn't get into McGill University.

HANS: Oh no! I'm sorry to hear that.

TOM: Yeah, and McGill was my first choice.

HANS: You must be disappointed. Did you apply to any other schools?

TOM: Yes, three other ones.

HANS: And?

TOM: I don't know yet. I'm waiting to hear back from them.

HANS: Well, good luck.

TOM: Thanks.

HANS: And if you want to talk, just call me.

TOM: Thanks, Hans. I really appreciate it.

B 🔁 Practice the conversation with a partner.

SPEAKING STRATEGY

C 🔁 Do the role play below with a partner. Practice responding to bad news and offering to help. Use the Useful Expressions and the conversation in **A** to help you.

Useful Expressions	
Responding to bad news	Offering to help
(I'm) sorry to hear that.	If you want to talk, (just) call me.
That's too bad.	If there's anything I can do,
How disappointing.	(just) let me know.
You must be disappointed.	

Student A: You just received an exam back. You didn't fail the test, but your grade is much lower than expected.

Student B: Respond to Student A's news, and offer to help.

D 🔁 Switch roles and do the role play again.

5 GRAMMAR

A Turn to page 203. Complete the exercises. Then do **B–E** below.

	Plans and Decisions with *be going to* and *will*		
	I'm / You're / He's / She's / We're / They're	(not)	**going to** go to Harvard.
Maybe	I / you / he / she / we / they	**will** **won't**	see a movie.

B 🔊 **Pronunciation: Reduced form of *going to*.** How do you pronounce *going to* in each sentence? Say the sentences aloud. Then listen and repeat. **CD 1 Track 38**

1. I'm going to consider taking a year off.

2. We're going to visit all of them.

3. She's going to write a recommendation.

4. You're going to have a great time!

C Circle the best answer for each item.

1. A: What are your plans for tonight?
   B: I'll / I'm going to study.

2. A: We need your application by 5:00 PM today.
   B: I'll / I'm going to do it right now.

3. A: When's the competition tomorrow?
   B: It'll / It's going to start at 9:00 AM.

4. A: What will you / are you going to do on your campus visit?
   B: Observe some classes.

5. A: What are your plans for this afternoon?
   B: Maybe I'll / I'm going to do some homework.

6. A: Who's writing your letter of recommendation?
   B: I'll / I'm going to ask Mr. Stuart, my math teacher.

D Imagine you can go to any school in the world. Choose a school and complete the sentences.

1. I'll apply to _____ schools.
   (number)

2. I'll go to _____.
   (name of school)

3. I'll live at / in _____.
   (home / a dorm room / my own apartment)

4. I'll study _____.
   (name of major)

5. I'll graduate in _____ years.
   (number)

6. After graduation, I'll become _____.
   (a / an + job)

E 🔄 Ask questions to get your partner's answers to **D**. On a piece of paper, write six questions with *be going to* and the question words below. Take turns asking and answering the questions with a partner.

> ℹ️ At the moment you are making a decision about the future, use *will*. Once you have made the decision, use *be going to*.

1. How many…?

2. Where…?

3. Where…?

4. What…?

5. When…?

6. What…?

6 COMMUNICATION

A The two questions in the chart ask about someone's future plans. Read the answers. Then complete each question with *be going to*. Check answers with a partner.

Yes / No questions	_____ study English this summer?	Yes, I am. / Maybe. / No, I'm not.
Wh- questions	What _____ do after graduation?	I'm going to take a trip.

B Read the questions on the left side of the chart. In the *Me* column, check (✔) the activities you're planning to do in the future. Then add your own question.

Are you going to...	Me	Classmate's name	Wh- Question	Answer
graduate from high school or college soon?			When...?	
take a trip somewhere this summer?			Where...?	
go out this weekend?			Who...?	
study after class today?			What...?	
take a test in English (like the TOEFL) soon?			Which...?	
keep studying English after this class?			Where...?	
_____?				

C Interview your classmates. For each question, find a different person who answers *yes*. Write the classmate's name in the chart above. Ask a *Wh-* question to get more details.

Are you going to study after class today?

Yes, I am.

Where are you going to study?

In the park.

D Look at the answers you got above. Which one was the most interesting? Tell the class.

1 VOCABULARY

A  The people below are college seniors or recent graduates. Take turns reading each opinion aloud with a partner.

"I want to <u>do an internship</u> this summer. **At some point** before then, I have to <u>create a résumé</u>." —Linh

"I'm going to <u>take time off</u> **in the near future**, maybe after graduation, and go on vacation." —Martina

"I'm working now, but **eventually**, I'd like to <u>go back to school</u> and get my PhD." —Roberto

"**Someday**, I'd like to <u>be my own boss</u>, but not yet. I have a lot to learn still." —Simon

Word Bank
Definite future time
after graduation
in a month
next year
this summer
Indefinite future time
soon
in a few days / weeks
in the near future
at some point
someday / eventually

B  Look at the underlined expressions in **A**. Answer the questions. Then tell a partner.

Which person wants to…

1. return to school? _____

2. work somewhere and learn to do a job? _____

3. work for himself? _____

4. not work or study for a short time? _____

5. create a summary of her education and job experience? _____

C  When do the people in **A** want to do these things? Do they give a definite future time or not? Tell a partner.

D  Look again at the underlined expressions in **A**. Do you want to do any of these things? If yes, when? Use the future time expressions to tell a partner.

2 LISTENING

A 🔊 **Listen for gist.** You are going to hear three different conversations. In each, which sentence is true? Listen and circle the best answer. **CD 1 Track 39**

1. a. She's going to graduate soon.

   b. She is applying to school.

   c. She just got accepted to a good school.

2. a. She's working on her résumé.

   b. She's going to be her own boss.

   c. She just got a new job.

3. a. She wants to take time off from college.

   b. She's planning to do an internship.

   c. She wants to change her major.

B 🔊 **Listen for details.** Read the sentences below. Then listen again. Write one word in each blank and circle the correct answers. **CD 1 Track 39**

Many people move to big cities such as New York after graduation.

Conversation 1

1. The woman wants to get a degree in _____.

2. She's planning to go this May / in the spring.

Conversation 2

3. The woman is going to do a(n) _____.

4. She's going to make money at some point / right away.

Conversation 3

5. The woman wants to _____ in New York.

6. She plans to do this after graduation / in the near future.

7. She will / won't return to regular classes in September.

Word Bank
A *paying position* is a job in which you make money.
A school year is divided into *terms* (for example, the spring and fall term).

C 🔄 Tell a partner: What are the women in each conversation doing or planning to do? Do you know anyone who did any of these things?

> The third woman wants to... My older brother is doing that now.

3 READING

A DIFFERENT ROAD TO SUCCESS

A 🔗 You have an idea for a new company. You think it will be successful. What should you do? Circle an answer. Then tell a partner.

   a. Get your college degree. After graduation, start your company.

   b. Skip (don't go to) college. Start your company right away.

B **Draw conclusions.** Read paragraphs 1–3 in the reading. How would Peter Thiel answer the question in **A**?

C **Infer meaning.** Find the words in **bold** in the reading. Write each word next to the correct definition.

   1. a teacher or advisor _____

   2. a chance to do something important or interesting _____

   3. did something uncertain or dangerous _____

   4. a hidden surprise or problem _____

D **Scan for details.** Find the statements below in paragraphs 1–3. Circle T for *True* and F for *False*. Correct the false statements.

Thiel fellows…

   1. can be any age.   T   F

   2. have to take classes for two years.   T   F

   3. work for free.   T   F

   4. work with special advisors.   T   F

   5. come from all over the world.   T   F

E 🔗 **Identify pros and cons.** What are the pros (good things) and cons (bad things) of being a Thiel fellow? Read paragraphs 4 and 5. Write your ideas on a piece of paper. Compare your answers with a partner's.

F 🔗 Answer the questions with a partner.

   1. What was Eden Full's project? Was she successful?

   2. In your opinion, is the Thiel Fellowship a good idea or not? Why?

1. When Eden Full was 20 years old, she did something unusual: She dropped out[1] of Princeton University. She had an idea for a new kind of technology, an inexpensive kind of solar panel.

2. Full **took a risk** and quit college to work on her idea, but she had help—not from her parents or friends but from billionaire entrepreneur[2] Peter Thiel. In 2010, he created a program called the Thiel Fellowship.[3] It helps people between the ages of 18 and 20 to work on a "big idea." Maybe they want to create a new kind of technology or medicine, or perhaps they want to solve an important social problem. The program gives these young people $100,000 to work on their project for two years. During this time, each person (now called a "fellow") also works with a **mentor**—a successful businessperson, scientist, or inventor. The mentors help the young entrepreneurs.

3. Each year, hundreds of people from around the world apply to the program, but only 20 are accepted. It's an exciting **opportunity**, but there is a **catch**. To be a Thiel fellow, a person must skip or drop out of college. This way, the person can work on his or her project only. He or she won't have to spend time in class or doing homework.

4. For Eden Full, this worked well. She started her project and then returned to Princeton two years later and got her degree. But some people worry about the Thiel Fellowship. Not everyone will be successful, they say. Some projects will fail, and some people won't go back to college.

5. Supporters of the Thiel Fellowship see it differently. The young entrepreneurs will learn a lot. They will also meet important leaders in business, science, and technology, and some will eventually get great jobs. Best of all, some projects will help others—like Eden Full's solar panels, which are now used in nine countries. The reality is this, say supporters: To be successful in life, you have to take risks at some point. Why wait until you're 35? Do it when you're 20.

[1] If you *drop out* of school, you stop going to school.
[2] An *entrepreneur* is a businessperson. Usually he or she starts a new company.
[3] A *fellowship* is a group of people. They share similar interests and work together.

4 GRAMMAR

A Turn to page 204. Complete the exercises. Then do **B** and **C** below.

Predictions with *be going to* and *will*
She**'s going to** / She **will** be very successful.
Some students **aren't going to** / **won't** pass the exam.
He <u>definitely</u> **won't** study history in college.
He**'ll** <u>probably</u> study business.
<u>Maybe</u> he**'ll** study economics, too.
A: **Is** she **going to** / **Will** she go to graduate school?
B: <u>Maybe</u>. / <u>Probably not</u>.

B Read about the two college students. Then think of questions to ask about their futures. Write the questions below.

Education: <u>Will Naomi get accepted to Stanford?</u>

<u>Is Alex going to…</u>

Job: _____

_____

Finances (money): _____

_____

Love life: _____

_____

Travel experience: _____

_____

C  Take turns asking and answering your questions with a partner. Explain your reasons. At least one answer should use a negative form.

> Will Naomi go back to Sydney someday?

> Yeah, probably. She liked it there.

Naomi is a straight-A student at a very good university. She wants to be a doctor someday. Last summer, she did an internship at a hospital in Sydney, Australia. She loved it there. In Sydney, she dated a guy named Alex, but after she returned home, they broke up. Recently, she applied to Stanford Medical School in the US. She hopes she will be accepted.

Alex is a college student from Sydney, Australia. He's also a talented musician. He's thinking about taking some time off from school. He wants to tour with his band around the world. He also misses his ex-girlfriend, Naomi. They broke up after she returned to her country.

5 WRITING

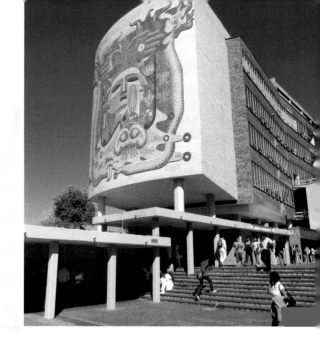

My name is Miguel Sanz. I am a student at the Universidad Nacional Autonoma de Mexico (UNAM) in Mexico City. This May, I am going to graduate with a degree in journalism. **In my third year at UNAM**, I did an internship at *El Universal*, one of Mexico's largest newspapers. There, I worked with senior reporters on different news stories. I also made changes to sports blogs on the paper's website. **In addition to my studies**, I enjoy playing sports, and at UNAM I am on the chess and swim teams. I also like learning languages, and I speak English and some Portuguese.

A Read the personal profile above. Then complete the outline about Miguel with a partner.

School: _____

Major: _____

Graduation date: _____

Work experience (when / where / what): _____

School activities: _____

Other abilities: _____

> **i** A personal profile is a short summary (about 100–150 words) of your school and work experience and your abilities.

B Complete the outline in **A** about yourself. The information you write can be real or invented. Then use your ideas and the example to write your own personal profile.

C Exchange papers with a partner.

1. Circle any mistakes. Then complete the outline in **A** about your partner on a separate piece of paper.

2. Return the paper to your partner. Make corrections to your own profile.

6 COMMUNICATION

A Your instructor is going to give you and a partner two classmates' profiles. Read them and make predictions about each person's future. Write your ideas on the paper.

Our predictions for you

Job:

Finances (money):

Family / Love life:

Travel experiences:

> We think you'll probably...
> or maybe you'll...

B Your instructor will now give you back your paper. Read the predictions you got. Tell a partner: Do you agree with them? Why or why not?

> The first prediction is: You'll probably study in the US at some point.
>
> Do you think that's true?
>
> Yeah, probably.

1 STORYBOARD

A 🔗 Ruben is talking to his teacher, Gina Walker. Complete the conversations.
Then tell a partner: Why does Ruben want to talk to Professor Walker?

Hello? This is Gina Walker.

Professor Walker? Hi, it's Ruben Vega. I'd _____ to _____ an appointment to see you this week.

Great. Can _____ come _____ tomorrow _____ 3:30?

3:30 – 4:30 Office Hours

I'm sorry, but that _____ doesn't _____ for me. Do you _____ anything _____?

Sure. _____ 4:30?

4:30

That's _____. See you then!

The next day in Professor Walker's office . . .

So, how can I help you today, Ruben?

Application

Well, I'm _____ to different business schools in London.

And I need a letter of _____ from a teacher.

Would you _____ writing one for me?

No. _____. You're an excellent student, Ruben!

B 🔗 Practice the conversations with a partner. Then change roles and practice again.

2 SEE IT AND SAY IT

A 🗩 Look at the neighborhood and discuss the questions with a partner. Take notes.

1. What are the people doing?

2. How are the people getting around?

3. How many pedestrians are there?

4. Does this look like a walkable neighborhood?

5. What places can you see in the picture?

6. What types of clothing are the people wearing?

B ♻ Tell another group about the scene.

3 I NEED YOUR ADVICE!

A Read the sentences. What advice would you give to someone who made these statements? Think about your answers.

1. I'm always late.

2. I forgot to bring today's English homework, and it's 25 percent of the class grade.

3. My parents don't like my friends.

4. It takes over two hours to get to school every day. I hate it.

5. I get really nervous when I have to talk to others in English.

6. I bought a new cell phone, and it's not working.

B Get into a group of three people. Write the numbers 1 to 6 on six small pieces of paper. Put the numbers in a bag or hat.

- When it's your turn, choose a number. Read aloud the problem in **A** that goes with your number. Explain the problem in more detail. Use your imagination.

- Your partners will listen and give you advice.

- Think about their suggestions. Which person gave you the best advice? Why?

4 BE GOING TO OR WILL?

A The chart shows the different uses of *be going to* and *will*. Complete the sentences below with *be going to* or *will*. Both may be correct in some sentences.

	To talk about plans you already made	To talk about a sudden decision	To make a general prediction about the future
be going to	✓		✓
will		✓	✓

1. Two weeks ago, I decided to take the TOEFL exam. I _____ take it next spring.

2. It's a beautiful evening. I think I _____ take a walk.

3. I bet there _____ be thousands of people at the free concert in the park tomorrow.

4. What _____ do this weekend? Do you have any plans?

5. A: The two o'clock movie is sold out, but we still have seats for the four o'clock show.
   B: OK, I _____ take two tickets for the show at 4:00.

6. She's really smart. I bet she _____ get accepted to a good school.

B Compare your answers with a partner's. Explain why you chose *be going to* or *will* in **A**.

5 LISTENING

A Read the poll below and choose your answer. Share your ideas with the class. What was the most common answer in your class?

POLL:

Do you think you'll get married?

a. Yes, definitely. I want to get married.
b. Yes, maybe someday, but I'm not sure when.
c. No, never. Marriage isn't for me.
d. I'm already married!

B A magazine asked a group of university students for their opinions on different topics. Listen and put the charts in the order (1–4) you hear them talked about. **CD 1 Track 41**

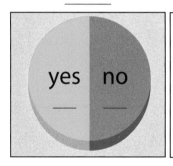  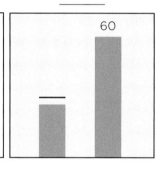 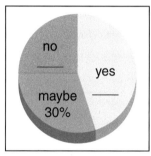

C Listen again and label the parts of each chart in **B** with the correct numbers or percentages. Some numbers will not be given. You have to guess them. **CD 1 Track 41**

D Look at your answers (1–4) in **B**. What do the students interviewed think? Read the sentences below and then choose the correct answer.

Chart 1: Over / Under 65% of the students think it's OK for couples with children to get divorced.

Chart 2: More students think studying abroad is good. The number dropped / rose.

Chart 3: Nearly / Exactly half of them think the university entrance exam is too difficult.

Chart 4: Around / Exactly three-fourths of them answered *Yes* or *Maybe* to this question: Do you think plastic surgery is OK?

E What do you think about the four opinions in **D**? Compare your ideas with a partner's. Explain your reasons.

I think it's OK for couples with children to get divorced.

Really? I'm afraid I disagree.

7 CELEBRATIONS

Look at the photo. Answer the questions.

1 What is this festival? What do people do?

2 Is there a festival like this in your country?

3 Look up the word *holiday* in your dictionary. What is an important holiday in your country?

UNIT GOALS

1 Invite someone to do something and accept or refuse an invitation

2 Agree with someone else

3 Describe different parties, festivals, and holidays

4 Talk about what people do on those days

People light lanterns and make wishes for good luck at a festival in Chiang Mai, Thailand.

Fans of the Colombian soccer team cheer for their team in Brazil.

1 **VIDEO** Soccer Celebrations

Word Bank
fan = person who enjoys something
inspiration = something that makes a person want to act
live = in person

A ▷ Look at the photo and the title of the video. Then watch the video and answer the question below.

The people in the video are watching an important sporting event. What event do you think it is?

_____

B ▷ Read questions 1–3 and guess the answers. Then watch again and write the answers you see and hear in the video.

1. Where do people watch big sporting events?

_____

2. When a favorite team wins an important game, why do people feel so happy?

_____

3. When their team scores a point, what do fans do?

_____

C 🔄 Answer the questions with a partner.

1. What was the last big sporting event you watched? Where did you watch it? Who won?

2. Are you a fan of any team? If yes, which one?

3. When you watch your team play, do you get emotional (do you yell or jump up and down)?

2 VOCABULARY

A  What do you know about an event called the Super Bowl? Take the quiz and find out! Compare your answers with a partner's. Check your answers at the bottom of the page.

1. The Super Bowl is the championship game for American football / soccer in the United States.

2. It is currently held on the first Monday / Sunday in February.

3. It is usually the most-watched television broadcast of the year in the US. More than ten million / one hundred million people watch it every year.

4. Not all of the TV viewers are football fans. Many watch to see the commercials / fireworks.

5. There is a big halftime show featuring famous athletes / singers.

B  Read the information about how people celebrate the Super Bowl. Answer the questions below. Then compare your answers with a partner's.

Many people **celebrate** the day by **throwing a party**. They **invite** friends to come to their home. Everyone **gets together** in the afternoon, and the game begins in the early evening.

> **Word Bank**
>
> **Word partnerships with *party***
>
> attend / go to / have / host / throw / organize / plan a party

Do you want to **have** your own Super Bowl **party**? Here is some advice on how to **plan** for it:

- **Decorate** your home or bake a cake with the teams' colors.
- Play games. Have your **guests** try and guess the final score of the game.
- Make sure you have enough seating for everyone. You may need to borrow extra chairs!
- Buy plenty of "finger foods"—things like chips and salsa. Chili is also good to cook for the **occasion**.
- Don't forget to **have a good time**!

1. When do people in your country throw a party? What occasion are they celebrating?

2. Who gets together on that day?

3. What special decorations are there? What foods are served for the occasion?

1. American football; 2. Sunday; 3. one hundred million; 4. commercials; 5. singers

3 LISTENING

A 🔊 **Listen for gist.** Two people are going to talk about an important celebration in their countries. Read the sentence. Then listen and complete it. **CD 2 Track 2**

Both speakers are talking about special days that celebrate _____.

    a. getting a driver's license

    b. graduating from college

    c. growing up

    d. getting married

B 🔊 **Listen for details.** Read the sentences below. Then listen and match each sentence with the correct celebration. Some sentences are true for both celebrations. **CD 2 Track 3**

The Rose Party: _____   **Coming of Age Day:** _a,_____

    a. You are 20.

    b. You are 15.

    c. It happens in Japan.

    d. It happens in El Salvador.

    e. It's only for young women.

    f. You wear special clothes.

    g. Everyone celebrates together on a day in January.

    h. There's a ceremony at City Hall first.

    i. There's a religious ceremony first.

    j. You get gifts.

    k. Many people come to your home to eat and dance.

    l. You go with friends to different clubs and parties.

C 🔄 **Summarize.** Choose one of the celebrations above. Use your answers in **A** and **B** and describe it to a partner.

D 🔄 Discuss the questions with a partner.

    1. Is there a similar celebration in your country?

    2. When is it held, and what happens on that day?

4 SPEAKING

A 🔊 🔁 **Pronunciation: Reduced *want to*.** Listen and complete the dialog. Notice the pronunciation of *want to*. Then practice the dialog with a partner. **CD 2 Track 4**

A: _____ do you _____ do this weekend?

B: I don't know. Maybe see that new sci-fi movie? _____ you _____ come with me?

A: Sorry, but I don't really _____ see that movie.

B 🔊 🔁 Listen to the conversation. Then answer the questions with a partner. **CD 2 Track 5**

1. Omar is going to a party. What kind of party is it? How does Omar invite Lane?

2. Does Lane accept? What does she say?

OMAR: Hey, Lane. My classmate Sayuri is having a party this weekend.

LANE: Really?

OMAR: Yeah, it's a costume party.

LANE: Sounds like fun.

OMAR: Do you want to go with me?

LANE: Are you sure? I don't really know Sayuri.

OMAR: No problem. She said I could invite a friend.

LANE: OK, then. I'd love to go. When exactly is it?

OMAR: On Saturday night.

LANE: Wow, that's the day after tomorrow! I need to get a costume.

OMAR: Me too. There's a good place near here that rents them. Let's go there after school.

LANE: Sounds good!

C 🔁 Practice the conversation with a partner.

SPEAKING STRATEGY

D On a piece of paper, write four invitations using the information in the box. Use the Useful Expressions to help you.

E 🔁 Take turns inviting your partner to the events in **D**. Refuse two of your partner's invitations. Give an excuse (a reason for saying "no").

come to my birthday party	study together	after class	tomorrow
see a movie	your idea: _____	this weekend	tonight

Useful Expressions		
Inviting someone to do something		**Accepting or refusing an invitation**
Do you want Would you like How'd you like	to go with me?	Sure, I'd love to. That sounds great. I'm sorry, but I can't. I have plans. Unfortunately, I can't. I have to work. I'd love to, but I'm busy (then / that day).
Speaking tip		
When refusing an invitation, it's polite to give a simple explanation.		

We have an English test this Friday.
How'd you like to study for it after class?   I'd love to, but...

5 GRAMMAR

A Turn to page 205. Complete the exercises. Then do **B–D** below.

Agreeing with Other People's Statements: *so*, *too*, *neither*, and *either*		
	Affirmative	**Negative**
With *be*	I'm going to Emi's party. **So** am I. / I am **too**. / Me **too**.	I'm not going to Emi's party. **Neither** am I. / I'm not **either**. / Me **neither**.
With other verbs	I have a costume for the party. **So** do I. / I do **too**. / Me **too**.	I don't have a costume for the party. **Neither** do I. / I don't **either**. / Me **neither**.

B Match each statement with a correct response.

1. I'm having a party this weekend.
2. The teacher wasn't there yesterday.
3. I missed the bus this morning.
4. I was late for my first class.
5. I didn't have a good time at the party.
6. Tim and Monica speak Spanish.

a. Neither was I.
b. Neither did I.
c. So do I.
d. So did I.
e. I was too.
f. So am I.

> *Me too* and *me neither* are common in casual spoken conversation.

C Complete the sentences. Make them true for you.

1. I like / I don't like to stay at home on the weekend.
2. I like / I don't like to talk during class.
3. I need / I don't need to study harder.
4. I think / I don't think big parties are fun.
5. I'm good at / I'm not good at remembering new vocabulary.

D Compare your opinions in **C** with a partner's.

I like to stay at home on the weekend.

So do I. What do you like to do?

Play games on my computer.

I like to stay at home on the weekend.

Really? Not me! I like to go out with my friends.

6 COMMUNICATION

A Plan a party with a partner. Choose a place or thing from each category or think of an idea of your own.

Type of party

a. a costume party

b. a pool party

c. a birthday party

Place

a. a friend's house

b. a nightclub

c. a park

Type of food

a. finger foods

b. barbecue

c. pasta salad

B Invite four other pairs to your party. Ask and answer questions about each others' parties. Complete the invitations below.

> Would you like to come to our party next week?

> What kind of party is it?

> It's a surprise birthday party for Antonio. He turns 22 next Friday.

Type of party: _____
Place: _____
Food: _____

Type of party: _____
Place: _____
Food: _____

Type of party: _____
Place: _____
Food: _____

Type of party: _____
Place: _____
Food: _____

C Discuss the parties in **B** with your partner. What do you think of each one? Choose your favorite party together and then share your choice with the class.

> I really like the surprise birthday party.

> So do I. The costume party sounds fun, too.

The International Festival of the Sahara takes place in December for four days in Douz, a village in Tunisia near the Sahara Desert. Thousands of people gather to celebrate the traditions of the desert people.

Events

- Watch people compete in different games to win prizes. Be sure to see one of the horse or camel races.

- Love words? Don't miss the festival's poetry competition.

- Local musicians and DJs from around the world perform every night.

- Participate in activities outside of Douz. Visit the dunes (large sand hills) for sand skiing and other sports.

1 VOCABULARY

A 🔁 Take turns reading the information about the festival aloud with a partner.

B Complete each definition with the correct form of a word or phrase in **blue**.

Word Bank		
Word Families		
Verb	**Noun**	**Noun (person)**
compete	competition	competitor
participate	participation	participant
perform	performance	performer

1. To play a game or other activity and try to be the best: _compete_

2. A type of activity (running, driving) that you try to be the fastest in: _____race_____

3. To sing, dance, or play music in front of others: _____

4. To come together in a group: _____

5. To happen: _____

6. Something (like money) given to the winner of a game or activity: _____

7. To join in and do something together with others: _____

8. The customs or ways of doing something for a long time: _____

C 🔁 Cover the information about the festival. Ask and answer the questions with a partner.

1. Where and when does the festival take place?

2. What happens at the festival?

2 LISTENING

Mount Cameroon is an active volcano.

A 🔊 **Listen for the main idea.** You will hear a news report about an event in the African country of Cameroon. Listen and answer the questions. **CD 2 Track 6**

CAMEROON

1. What event is the reporter talking about?

   a. a musical performance

   b. a big competition

   c. a special parade

2. What is the event called? Write the word.

   The ___Race___ of Hope

B 🔊 **Listen for details.** Listen and complete the notes about the event. **CD 2 Track 7**

1. When the event takes place: every year, usually in __Feb__

2. Number of participants this year: ___400___ people

3. Distance: about ___40___ kilometers

4. What people do: They run up a ___m___ and then back down.

5. Prize: over $ _____

6. Other events: During the weekend, there's also a _____.

C 🔊 🔄 **Draw conclusions.** Think about the name of this event. Why do you think it has this name? Listen again and write your answer. Then compare your ideas with a partner's. **CD 2 Track 7**

_____

D 🔄 Imagine you and your partner work for an advertising agency. You are helping the government of Cameroon tell the world about this special event. Create a print or video advertisement about the event. Use your notes in **A–C**.

E 👥 Share your advertisement with two other pairs. Which one is the best?

3 READING

A 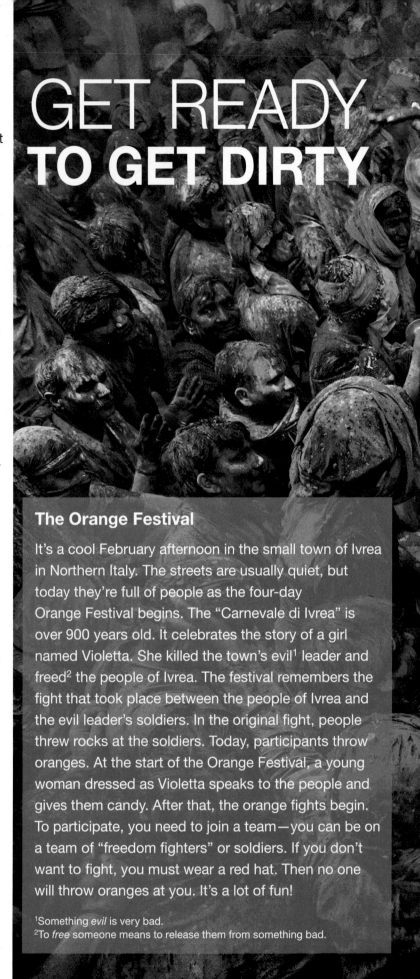 **Make predictions; Draw conclusions.** Read the title and look at the photo. What do you think happens at this festival? Tell a partner.

B **Read for details.** Work with a partner. Answer questions 1–3 about your festival only.

Student A: Read about the Orange Festival.

Student B: Read about the Festival of Color.

1. Where and when does it take place?
2. What is the purpose of the festival? What event does it celebrate?
3. What do people do at the festival?

C Ask your partner the questions in **B** about his or her festival. Then read about the festival. Check your partner's answers.

D **Scan for details; Categorize information.** What festival is each sentence about? Write *O* for Orange Festival and *H* for Holi. Write *B* if both answers are possible.

_____ 1. It's celebrated in different countries.
_____ 2. It's about an old story.
_____ 3. It celebrates good over bad.
_____ 4. You throw things at other people.
_____ 5. You need to join a team.
_____ 6. The day before, people light a fire.

E Answer the questions with a partner.

1. Imagine you can go to Holi or the Orange Festival. Which one do you want to go to? Why?
2. Are there any old, traditional festivals in your country? Answer the questions in **B** about them. Do you like them?

GET READY TO GET DIRTY

The Orange Festival

It's a cool February afternoon in the small town of Ivrea in Northern Italy. The streets are usually quiet, but today they're full of people as the four-day Orange Festival begins. The "Carnevale di Ivrea" is over 900 years old. It celebrates the story of a girl named Violetta. She killed the town's evil[1] leader and freed[2] the people of Ivrea. The festival remembers the fight that took place between the people of Ivrea and the evil leader's soldiers. In the original fight, people threw rocks at the soldiers. Today, participants throw oranges. At the start of the Orange Festival, a young woman dressed as Violetta speaks to the people and gives them candy. After that, the orange fights begin. To participate, you need to join a team—you can be on a team of "freedom fighters" or soldiers. If you don't want to fight, you must wear a red hat. Then no one will throw oranges at you. It's a lot of fun!

[1]Something *evil* is very bad.
[2]To *free* someone means to release them from something bad.

The Festival of Color

The Festival of Color, also called Holi, is a popular spring celebration. It takes place every year, usually in early or mid March, in India and other countries like Nepal and Sri Lanka. In Indian mythology,[3] an evil woman tried to kill a young man named Prahlad by burning him in a fire. Because Prahlad was a good person, he escaped[4] from the fire unhurt. Today, people remember this event by lighting large fires in the streets on the night before Holi. The fire is a symbol[5] of the end of all bad things. The next day, Holi, celebrates the start of spring and a new beginning. To celebrate, people gather in the streets. They throw colored powder into the air and say "Holi Hai!" Others throw colored water or powder at each other. By the end of the festival, the streets are filled with color and smiles!

[3]*Mythology* is a collection of very old traditional stories.
[4]If you *escape* from something bad, you get away from it.
[5]A *symbol* is something that represents something else. For example, a picture of a heart is a symbol of love.

4 GRAMMAR

A Turn to page 206. Complete the exercises. Then do **B** and **C** below.

Time Clauses with *before, after, when*	
Time clause	**Main clause**
Before the festival starts,	Violetta speaks.
After the party ended,	we went home.
When you throw powder in the air,	you say "Holi Hai!"
Main clause	**Time clause**
Violetta speaks	**before** the festival starts.
We went home	**after** the party ended.
You say "Holi Hai!"	**when** you throw powder in the air.

B 🔄 Look at the photo. Then read about Paloma's activities on Three Kings' Day. With a partner, combine the different sentences using *before*, *after*, and *when*. Multiple answers are possible.

On January 6, people around the world celebrate Three Kings' Day. In Spain and many Latin American countries, children get presents and families eat a special meal together.

January 5

9:00 PM   Paloma and her family go to the Three Kings' Parade.

January 6

7:00 AM   Paloma's younger brothers get up.

7:00 AM   They wake Paloma up.

7:15 AM   The family gathers in the living room.

7:20 AM   They open presents.

8:00 AM   Everyone relaxes and enjoys the morning.

11:00 AM   Paloma and her mom prepare lunch.

2:00 PM   Paloma's grandparents arrive at her house. Everyone has lunch.

3:00 PM   The family eats a special sweet bread called a *roscón*.

3:30 PM   The adults talk and the children play games.

When Paloma's brothers get up, they...

C 🔄 Think of a holiday you know. What happens on this day? Use *after*, *before*, and *when* to describe the day's events. Tell a partner.

5 WRITING

A 🔄 Read the paragraphs on the right. Then tell a partner:

1. Is the person writing about a festival or holiday?

2. What is it called?

3. Where and when does it happen?

4. What do people do, and when?

B What is an important holiday or festival in your city or country? Use the questions in **A** to make some notes. Then use your ideas and the example to help you write a paragraph or two about it.

C 🔄 Exchange papers with a partner. Answer the questions in **A** about your partner's writing. Circle any mistakes. Then return the paper to your partner. Make corrections to your own paper.

In Korea, we have a holiday called *Chuseok*. It usually takes place in September or early October. It is a holiday for giving thanks and remembering our ancestors.

Many people travel to their hometowns to spend Chuseok with their families. Every family celebrates Chuseok a little differently. In my family, we prepare traditional foods a day or two before Chuseok. On Chuseok morning, my family does a special ceremony to remember our ancestors. After this, we have a big meal, and we give each other small gifts. In the evening, we have a nice dinner. After the meal, we play games or watch TV. There are lots of fun TV shows on during Chuseok!

6 COMMUNICATION

A 🔄 Look at these unusual holidays. Then ask and answer the questions below with a partner.

World Tourism Day
September 27

National Men Make Dinner Day
the first Thursday of November

1. What do you think happens on each day?

2. Which one(s) would you like to celebrate? Why?

B 🔄 With your partner, use the questions to invent an unusual holiday.

- What is the name of the holiday?
- When does the holiday take place?
- What is the reason for the holiday?
- Who celebrates it?

- What do people do on the holiday?
- Do people celebrate it at home or outside the home?
- What do people wear?
- Are there any special foods or decorations?

C 🔄 Present your holiday to the class. When you listen, take notes and answer the questions in **B**.

D 🔄 Review your notes. In your opinion, which holiday is the most interesting? Tell the class.

8 STORYTELLING

A group of friends tell stories around a campfire in Yosemite National Park, California, the United States.

Look at the photo. Answer the questions.

1 Where are the people? What are they doing?

2 What kind of stories do you think they are telling?

3 Look up *fairy tale* in your dictionary. What is a famous fairy tale you know? What happens in the story?

UNIT GOALS

1 Describe a story and explain why people like or don't like it

2 Use transitions to keep a story going

3 Talk about fairy-tale characters and what stories mean

4 Describe how something is done

People dress up as the characters Princess Leia and the stormtroopers from the original *Star Wars* movie.

to get on ≠ to get off

1 VIDEO Star Wars Subway Car

A Look at the photo. Who are these characters? What do you know about them and about the movie *Star Wars*? Discuss with a partner.

B Watch the video. Then answer the questions with a partner.

1. Where are the people?   2. What are they doing?

C Watch the video again. Put the events in order.

_3_ Stormtroopers get on the subway.   _2_ Princess Leia reads a book.

_5_ Darth Vader gets on the subway.   _7_ Everyone gets off the subway.

_1_ Princess Leia gets on the subway.   _4_ A stormtrooper grabs Princess Leia.

_6_ Darth Vader and Princess Leia argue.

D Answer the questions with a partner.

1. Who are the people under the costumes? Why are they acting out the *Star Wars* story?

2. The people on the subway are enjoying the *Star Wars* characters. How would you feel if you saw these characters in public?

2 VOCABULARY

made-up → fantasy / not real.

make-up →] crime una historia
] mentir

A 🔄 With a partner, read about two popular TV shows. Which show is more interesting? Why?

	Game of Thrones (fantasy drama)	*True Detective* (crime drama)
The story	**It tells the story of** three royal families fighting for control of a **made-up** world.	**The story is about** a small team of detectives solving one major crime.
The setting	It takes place hundreds of years ago in a made-up land.	It takes place in the modern-day United States. *→ to happen*
The cast	It has one of the largest casts of **characters** on television.	It has a small cast of main characters, and they change every season.
Where the idea came from	It's **based on** a popular **fantasy** book series.	It's created and written by one man.
Why fans say they like it	The characters are exciting to watch, and the story is **unpredictable**.	The quality of the acting is very high, and the story is **realistic**.
Why others say they don't like it	There are too many characters, and the story is **hard to follow**.	The story is too **violent**.

B 🔄 Now think of your favorite TV show. Answer the questions about it on a separate piece of paper. Then tell a partner.

1. What's the name of the show? _____

2. Who are the main characters? _____

3. Where does it take place? _____

4. Is it based on anything? _____

5. What's the story about? _____

_____

6. How would you describe the story?

predictable / unpredictable   easy / hard to follow

realistic / unrealistic   your idea: _____

Word Bank
Word partnerships with *story*
The story is about… / It tells the story of…
a character <u>in</u> a story
tell a story
make up a story

Game of Thrones takes place in a made-up land populated by dragons and other imaginary creatures.

3 LISTENING

A 🔁 **Infer information.** Answer the questions. Take notes and share your ideas with a partner.

Word Bank
contribute = give something to help someone

1. Have you ever heard the word *crowdsourcing* in English?

2. Can you guess the meaning by looking at the two parts of the word: *crowd* and *source*?

B 🔊 **Listen for details.** Listen to the conversation about how crowdsourcing is used to write a story. Circle the correct answer to complete each sentence. **CD 2 Track 9**

1. Jamal is working _____.
   a. alone
   b. with a couple of friends
   (c.) with a lot of people

2. Jamal met the other writers _____.
   a. at school
   b. in writing class
   (c.) online

3. Each person suggests _____ for the story.
   a. a character
   (b.) a sentence
   c. an ending

4. The story is _____.
   (a.) unpredictable
   b. unrealistic
   c. hard to follow

5. Jamal is working on a _____ story.
   a. fantasy
   b. love
   (c.) crime

6. The story isn't _____.
   a. realistic
   (b.) true
   c. well known

C 🔁 Look at your notes in **A** and your answers in **B**. What is a crowdsourced story? Complete the summary below. Compare your answers with a partner's.

Part of Jamal's story takes place in Madrid. What place do you think would make a good story setting?

To create a crowdsourced story, (1.) _People_ work together. They don't work in an office. They work (2.) _online_. Everyone contributes (3.) _with one (sentence)_.

→ sentence

The people don't (4.) _know_ each other, and they don't receive any (5.) _money_ for their work.

D 🔁 Discuss the questions with a partner.

1. Do you think crowdsourcing is good or bad?

2. Do you think crowdsourcing is a good way to tell a story?

WORLD LINK Crowdsourcing is used for business and marketing purposes, to solve math or science riddles, and more. Go online and find another interesting way that crowdsourcing is used.

4 SPEAKING

A 🔊 **Pronunciation: Compound words.** Here are more words used to describe stories. Look up the ones you don't know in your dictionary. Then listen and repeat. Pay attention to the stress. **CD 2 Track 10**

1. heartbreaking   2. heartwarming   3. uplifting — _INSPIRADOR_

B 🔊 Mia is telling Nico a story. Listen and then answer the questions about the story. **CD 2 Track 11**

1. How many characters are in the story? ⌐
2. Where does it take place? _RESTAURANT_
3. What happened? Was the story easy to follow?
4. This is an example of a *feel-good* story. What do you think that means?

MIA: Wow, I just heard an amazing story.

NICO: Yeah? What's it about?

MIA: It's a story about a waitress. She had a lot of money problems.

NICO: That sounds hard.

MIA: It is. Anyway, she found out she was losing her apartment. She had to move, but she didn't have enough money.

NICO: Oh no!

MIA: As it turns out, she told one of her customers about the situation. This customer was special. He came to the restaurant often and knew the waitress well. And he wanted to help her.

NICO: So what did he do?

MIA: One day he paid his bill and left the restaurant, as usual. When the waitress went to collect her tip, she found a $3,000 tip... on a bill of $43.50!

NICO: Are you serious?

MIA: I am. It's a true story. And in the end, the waitress was OK.

NICO: What a heartwarming story. I'm glad it had a happy ending.

> ℹ️ When eating out in North America, it is customary to tip your server an extra 20 percent for service after you have finished eating your meal.

C 🔄 Practice the conversation with a partner.

SPEAKING STRATEGY

D 🔄 On a piece of paper, write a word or single sentence for each item below. Then exchange papers with a partner. Use your partner's notes and the Useful Expressions to write a story.

1. a person's name
2. another person's name
3. a place
4. how the two people met
5. what happened to the two people

Useful Expressions
Keeping a story going
One day,…
So, (then),…
Later,…
After that,…
As it turns out,…
It turns out that,…

E 🔄 Work with a new partner and do the following:

Student A: Tell your story.

Student B: Listen. Tell your partner what you liked about the story.

> My story is about a student named Jonah. Something amazing happened to him.

F 🔄 Switch roles and do **E** again.

> What happened?

5 GRAMMAR

A Turn to page 207. Complete the exercises. Then do **B** and **C** below.

The Past Continuous Tense: Statements				
Subject	*was / were (not)*	**Verb + *ing***		
I / He / She	was(n't)	**studying**	English	at four o'clock. last summer. after lunchtime.
You / We / They	were(n't)			

The Past Continuous Tense: Questions						
	Wh- word	*was / were*	**Subject**	**Verb + *ing***		**Answers**
Yes / No Questions		Were	you	**reading**	a story?	Yes, I was. / No, I wasn't.
Wh- Questions	What	were	you	**reading**?		(I was **reading**) a story.

B Unscramble the questions and their answers.

1. were / doing / at / what / you / last night / 8:00 _____

   Game of Thrones / watching / I / on TV / was _____

2. yesterday / friend / was / what / wearing / best / your _____

   _____

   wearing / school / her / she / uniform / was _____

3. your / were / phone / talking / earlier / you / cell / on _____

   _____

   wasn't / no, / I _____

   lunch / was / I / eating _____

4. studying / was / your / yesterday / class / what _____

   were / *World Link* / grammar / we / studying / in _____

5. summer / family / was / your / traveling / last _____

   were / we / yes, _____

   to / went / Spain / we _____

C 🔄 Ask and answer the questions in **B** with a partner. Give answers that are true for you. Then think of a follow-up question to ask a partner.

> What were you doing last night at 8:00?

> How long were you studying?

> I was studying at home in my room.

> For about three hours. I was preparing for a big test.

6 COMMUNICATION

A 🔊 You are going to hear two people talk about a car accident. One person is lying. Listen to each person's story and take notes below. **CD 2 Track 12**

	Jenna	Ryan
When did it happen?		
Where did it happen?		
What happened?		
What color was the car?		
Who was driving?		

B 🔁 Circle your answers below. Discuss your ideas with a partner.

1. Jenna / Ryan remembers the details clearly.

2. Jenna / Ryan sounds more confident.

3. Jenna / Ryan hesitates more.

4. I think Jenna / Ryan is making up the story.

C 🔁 Think about something funny or unusual that happened to you. Then follow the steps below with a partner.

1. **Student A:** Tell your story.
   Student B: Listen and take notes on *who, what, where, when,* and *why.*

2. Switch roles and repeat step 1.

3. Now choose <u>one</u> of your stories.

4. Think of ways that you can make the story untrue, for example, changing the details. Write down another version of the story with the untrue parts.

D 👥 Get together with another pair.

- **Pair 1:** One of you will tell the story as it really happened to you. The other person will tell the story with the made-up parts. Begin with each person saying one sentence of their story. Take turns telling the rest of the story, one sentence at a time.

- **Pair 2:** Ask each person in Pair 1 questions about their story. You have one minute. Then guess: Who is telling the truth and who is making up the story? How do you know?

> I was walking to work one day when I met someone famous.

> *I* was walking to the store one day when I met someone famous.

> OK, let me start with Person 1. You said you were walking to work. Where exactly do you work?

E 👥 Switch roles and do **D** again.

The Hunger Games is a modern fairy tale. The main character is brave and overcomes many challenges on her journey.

In most modern fairy tales...

1. there is a good character and a bad character.
2. the good character is often **clever** and brave.
3. the good character **struggles** to do something difficult (like escape from a dangerous situation and **survive**).
4. **incredible** things happen (animals talk, ghosts appear).
5. the good character **overcomes** the difficult situation and succeeds.
6. the good character often **discovers** something important about life.
7. the story usually ends happily.

[handwritten: overcome = superar]

1 VOCABULARY *[handwritten: struggle = luta]*

A 👥 The movie in the photo is an example of a modern fairy tale. Can you guess why? Tell a partner. Then take turns reading sentences 1–7 aloud.

B Match the correct form of each word in **blue** in sentences 1–7 with a definition below.

1. to deal with a difficult situation successfully ___overcome___
2. intelligent ___clever___
3. to learn something you didn't know in the past ___discover___
4. hard to believe ___incredible___
5. to try hard to do something difficult ___struggle___
6. to stay alive in a difficult situation ___survive___

C 👥 Work with a partner. Follow the steps below.

1. Choose a modern fairy tale to talk about.
2. Are sentences 1–7 true about the story? Explain.
3. Do you like the story? Why or why not?
4. Switch roles and repeat 1–3.

Examples of modern fairy tales

The Hunger Games   *Star Wars*

Harry Potter   Your idea: _____

> In *The Hunger Games*, Katniss Everdeen is the good character. She's clever and brave. For example...

[handwritten: brave = courageous] *[handwritten: to overcome = to surpass]*

[handwritten: survival = sobrevivência] *[handwritten: survivor = sobrevivente]*

2 LISTENING

turtle = vive na água

lebre = a hare

a tortoise — *vive na terra*

A 🎧 **Build background knowledge; Make predictions.** Answer the questions with a partner.

1. What do the words in the box below mean?

2. Which words do you think describe the animals in the picture?

> arrogant   patient   quick   slow

3. Do you know the story of the tortoise and the hare?

fable = tábula

B 🔊 **Listen for main ideas.** Marnie and her dad are talking. Read the sentences. Then listen and circle the correct answer(s). **CD 2 Track 13**

1. There's a (contest) / game / test at school, and Marnie thinks she's going to fail / (lose) / win.

2. Laura Sanders is Marnie's friend / (competitor) / teacher.

3. Laura is very (talented) / funny / kind.

C 🔊 **Listen for details.** Marnie's dad tells her the story *The Tortoise and the Hare*. Listen and write *H* for hare and *T* for tortoise. **CD 2 Track 14**

1. The __H__ challenges the __T__.

2. The __H__ thinks he will win the race.

3. The __H__ takes a rest during the race.

4. The __T__ finishes the race first.

5. The __H__ was arrogant.

6. The __T__ was clever.

D 🔊 **Summarize.** Listen again. Marnie's dad is giving her some advice by telling the story. What is his advice? Listen again. Then list your ideas. **CD 2 Track 14**

Marnie's dad gives her this advice: ___rigth a good speech, overcome your shyness, be patient, work hard and practice a lot___

E 🎧 Answer the questions with a partner.

1. Why does Marnie's dad tell her the story?

2. Do you agree with her dad's advice?

3. Can you think of another old or traditional story that can still "teach a lesson" about life?

finally = eventually

3 READING

A 🔁 **Use background knowledge.**
Look at the title and the photo. What do you know about the fairy-tale character Cinderella? Tell a partner.

B **Identify main ideas.** Read the passage. Then write the headers below in the correct places in the reading. Two are extra.

2. One story, many cultures

Cinderella in the movies

4. Why we love her

3. A present-day Cinderella

The African Cinderella

1. A famous fairy tale

C **Scan for details.** Match the names (1–5) with the answers (a–f) to make true sentences. One answer is extra.

1. The African Cinderella ___c___
2. Becan ___d___
3. Cindy Ella ___f___
4. The Filipina Cinderella ___b___
5. Settareh ___a___

a. attends a New Year's party.
b. has a forest spirit help her.
c. has only one stepsister.
d. is a boy "Cinderella."
e. was a movie version of the Cinderella story.
f. is an unpopular high school student.

D 🔁 Answer the questions with a partner.

1. Why is the Cinderella story so popular? The reading lists three reasons. Do you agree with them?

2. Is there a Cinderella story in your country? If so, what is the story?

THE CINDERELLA STORY

1. ___A famous fairy tale___

The Cinderella story is a famous one. Cinderella was living happily with her family when her mother died. Her father remarried. Cinderella's new stepmother and two stepsisters treated her poorly. She had to wear old clothes and work hard while the sisters wore beautiful clothes and had fun.

You know the rest of the story. A good fairy[1] helped Cinderella. She turned Cinderella's old clothes into a beautiful dress. Cinderella went to a party, and a prince fell in love with her. Cinderella left the party quickly and didn't tell the prince her name. But she did leave a glass slipper, and the prince used that to find her. Eventually, Cinderella and the prince married and lived happily ever after.

2. ___One story, many cultures___

That's one telling of the story, but the Cinderella fairy tale is found in many different countries with some differences. In an African version, for example, there is one stepsister, not two. In a version from the Philippines, a forest spirit helps the Cinderella character. Settareh, a Middle Eastern Cinderella, goes to a New Year's party. And Cinderella is not always a woman. In an Irish story, a young boy, Becan, marries a princess and lives happily ever after.

3. ___A present-day Cinderella___

There are also modern retellings of the Cinderella story. In one, a girl named Cindy Ella is a student at a Los Angeles high school. Her fashionable stepmother and older stepsisters care a lot about shopping and money. Cindy doesn't. When she writes a letter to her school newspaper against a school dance, she becomes very unpopular with both students and teachers. Only her two best friends— and later the school's most handsome boy—support her.

4. ___Why we love her___

Why is the Cinderella story so popular and found in so many cultures? There are a few reasons. First of all, it's a romantic story, which is a popular style. Also, Cinderella is a kind girl with a hard life. People want her to succeed. But maybe the most important reason is that in the Cinderella story, a person struggles, but overcomes the difficulties in the end. That's a story that everyone—boy or girl, young or old—wants to believe can happen.

[1]A *fairy* is a person with magical power.

Cinderella and the prince dance at the party.

GRAMMAR

A Turn to page 209. Complete the exercises. Then do **B–E** below.

Adverbs of Manner	
Cinderella smiled **shyly** at the prince.	**Adverbs of manner** describe how something is done. Many end in *-ly,* and they often come after a verb.
He opened <u>the door</u> **quietly**. She answered <u>the question</u> **correctly**.	When there is <u>an object</u> (a noun or pronoun) after the verb, the adverb usually comes at the end of the sentence.
She was <u>different</u> from other children. You seem <u>unhappy</u>.	<u>Adjectives</u>, not adverbs, come after stative verbs (words like *be, have, hear, know, seem*).
She drives too **fast**. He studied **hard** for the exam. They didn't do **well** in school.	Some adverbs of manner don't end in *-ly.*

B Circle the adjective or adverb to complete the profile. Then take turns reading the story aloud with a partner.

As a child in the UK, Daniel Tammet was different / differently from other children. As a boy, he liked to play alone and acted strange / strangely around others. In school, he struggled to do good / well. To many of his classmates, Daniel seemed unusual / unusually, and they laughed at him. This hurt Daniel deep / deeply, and he became very shy / shyly.

As a teenager, Daniel discovered he had an incredible ability. He could solve difficult math problems almost instant / instantly. He also discovered another talent: he could learn to speak a language very quick / quickly. Today, he is fluent / fluently in ten languages.

As an adult, Daniel overcame his shyness. He wrote three books in which he speaks eloquent / eloquently about his life and ideas.

C Take turns asking and answering the questions with a partner.

1. As a child, how did Daniel act? Why?

2. How did people treat Daniel? How did this make him feel?

3. What two special abilities does Daniel have?

4. Does Daniel's story end happily? Why or why not?

D Get into a small group. Add four verbs and two adverbs to the chart.

E Choose a verb and an adverb. Then act out the combination. Can your group guess what you're doing? Take turns with the people in your group.

> **Word Bank**
>
> An *eloquent* speaker talks in a clear and powerful way.

Verbs		Adverbs	
climb	talk	calmly	patiently
dance	_____	carefully	quietly
laugh	_____	gracefully	terribly
run	_____	happily	_____
sing	_____	nervously	_____

> You're singing terribly!

5 WRITING

A Look at the picture from the Cinderella story. Answer the questions with a partner.

1. Who are the characters?
2. Where are they?
3. How do you think each person feels?

B Imagine it is the day after the party. Choose a character from the picture. Write an email in that character's words to a friend about the party. You can make up information, including other characters. See the example to the right. In your message, write at least eight sentences. Use three adverbs of manner. Also pay attention to your use of the simple past and past continuous tenses.

C Exchange papers with a partner. Did he or she follow the directions in **B**? Circle any mistakes. Then give the paper back to your partner.

Last night, my parents had a big party at a hotel downtown for my father's friends and coworkers. I didn't want to go, but I had to. At first, the party was incredibly boring. I waited patiently for an hour, and then I decided to leave. But then, when I was walking out, an amazing girl arrived and the whole night changed...

6 COMMUNICATION

A Work in a small group. One person begins. Read your message from Writing **B** to the group. Act it out with feeling. When you listen, guess: Who is the speaker?

B Were the stories with the same characters from **A** the same or different? Which one did you like the most?

Astronauts test a vehicle in the desert in Arizona in the United States.

Look at the photo. Answer the questions.

1 What job do these people do?

2 Would a job like this be interesting to you? Why or why not?

3 A *dream job* is an ideal or perfect job. What is your dream job?

UNIT GOALS

1 Describe a job

2 Discuss the qualities needed to do a job well

3 Practice a job interview

4 Talk about how long something has happened

1 **VIDEO** Job Interview Advice

A 🔄 This video gives advice for going on a job interview. Look up the expression *break the ice*. What is a good way to break the ice in an interview? Tell a partner.

B 🔄 Read the job interview tips from the video. Guess the answers with a partner. For some items, both answers are possible.

1. You should be in the building ___15___ minutes before your interview.
   a. 15   b. 30

2. ___a / b___ is important.
   a. The handshake   b. Eye contact

3. Be ready to answer when the interviewer says, "Tell me about your ___a / b___."
   a. goals   b. background

4. Go into the interview with a clear ___b___.
   a. question   b. goal

5. The most important piece of advice is to ___a___.
   a. know your audience   b. try not to make mistakes

6. When you apply for a creative job, don't ___b___.
   a. ask too many questions   b. overdress for the interview

7. The final advice is to ___b___.
   a. talk about your best work   b. be confident

C ▶ Watch the video. Check your answers in **B**.

D 🔄 Think of one more piece of job interview advice. Tell a partner.

responsible for

2 VOCABULARY

A  Read about the job. Then tell a partner: could you be a paramedic? Why or why not?

I'm a paramedic. I give medical help in an emergency. You have to be **responsible** to do this job. Each day is different, so you have to be **flexible**, too.

I report to work at 5:30 AM. I'm a **punctual** person, so the early start isn't a problem.

Some people work **independently**, but not me. I'm part of a team that includes a driver and a doctor. The driver knows the most **efficient** ways to get around, and the doctor is **knowledgeable** about medical problems.

Our team tries to approach people in a **personable** manner, even if they are confused or angry. And when people are injured, we are **cautious** when moving them into the ambulance.

This is a good job for someone who likes to take risks. I'm pretty **adventurous**. People also say I'm **courageous** to face these dangerous situations. I say I'm just doing my job.

A paramedic works in an ambulance and provides emergency medical care.

B Complete the Word Bank with the words in blue in **A**.

C 🔁 Answer the questions with a partner.

1. What is the hardest thing about being a paramedic?

2. What other jobs require you to be courageous? personable? flexible?

3. Which words in **A** describe you?

Word Bank

Similar / Same Meaning

changes easily → _flexible_
careful → _cautious_
brave → _courageous_
likes risk → _adventurous_
intelligent → _knowledgeable_
friendly → _personable_
on time → _punctual_
quick / easy → _efficient_
dependable → _responsible_
by yourself → _independently_

handwritten annotations:

to be on time
FRIENDLY / NICE
CAUTION

PERSONABLE = FRIENDLY
TO BE OF VALUE =
NERVE-WRECKING EXPERIENCE =
IT SPEAKS VOLUMES = TELL A LOT ABOUT YOU / PRIMEIRA IMPRESSÃO
THERE'S A LOT AT STAKE = HÁ MUITO EM RISCO / HÁ MUITO EM JOGO
JOB SEEKERS = JOB HUNTER (JOB HUNTING)
TO ARTICULATE YOUR AMBITIONS = DIZER EXATAMENTE O Q. QUER NO TRABALHO
A POTENTIAL EMPLOYER =
A JACK OF ALL TRADES = "FAZ TUDO"

A LITTLE STICKY = { ISSUE / UNCOMFORTABLE
UNRULY = NOT COOPERATING

3 LISTENING

A 🔄 **Use background knowledge.** Look at the jobs below. What are the most challenging aspects of each job? Tell your partner.

taxi driver	flight attendant	travel writer

B 🔊 **Infer information.** You will hear a man talking about his job. Listen. Which job in **A** does he do? Circle it. What information helped you choose your answer? **CD 2 Track 16**

C 🔊 **Make and check predictions.** What are the challenges of this job?

1. Read the statements in the chart. Try to guess the answers.

2. Listen and complete the statements. Use one word in each blank. **CD 2 Track 17**

Challenges
1. You're ___away___ from ___home___ a lot—about ___20___ days a month.
• It's hard to have a ___social___ life.
2. The job is hard on your ___health___.
• You ___stavid___ a lot.
• It's difficult to get enough ___sleep___ and to ___eat___ right.
3. Sometimes there's a ___rude___ person, but you still have to be friendly.
• It's not easy to stay ___calm___.
4. Sometimes a flight is ___late___, and people get ___angry___.
5. You meet some ___interesting___ people and get to ___visit___ a lot of places.

D 🔊 Listen to the sentences. Circle the quality that they describe. **CD 2 Track 18**

1. cautious   knowledgeable   flexible

2. courageous   personable   independent

3. adventurous   punctual   efficient

E 🔄 Discuss these questions with a partner.

1. The speaker talked about many of the challenges of his job. What are some of the good points of the job?

2. Would you like to do this job? Why or why not?

Archaeologists travel the world looking for clues about ancient cultures.

WORLD LINK

Think of another job where you get to travel a lot or meet people from around the world. Do research on the job and describe it to the class.

4 SPEAKING

A 🔊 Read the job ad. Then listen to Ines's interview. Is she the right person for the job? Why or why not? **CD 2 Track 19**

SIMON: So, Ines, tell me a little about yourself.

INES: Well, I'm a first-year student at City University, and I'm majoring in journalism.

SIMON: And you're working for your school's online newspaper, right?

INES: Yeah. I write a blog. It focuses on pop culture, fashion, music—stuff like that.

SIMON: How long have you worked there?

INES: For about six months. I post an entry once a week.

SIMON: Excellent. But if you work here, you'll need to post every Tuesday and Friday—by noon.

INES: No problem. I'm very punctual.

SIMON: Great. Now, we need someone right away. When can you start?

INES: On Monday.

SIMON: Perfect. Let me talk to my boss, and I'll be in touch with you later this week.

B 🔄 Practice the conversation in **A** with a partner.

SPEAKING STRATEGY

Useful Expressions: Interviewing for a Job		
	The interviewer	The applicant
Starting the interview	Thanks for coming in today.	It's great to be here. / My pleasure.
Discussing abilities and experience	Tell me a little about yourself.	I'm a first-year university student. I'm majoring in journalism.
	Can you (work independently)? Are you (punctual)?	Yes, I can. For example,... Yes, I am. For example,...
	Do you have any experience (writing a blog)?	Yes, I write one for my school newspaper now.
Ending the interview	Do you have any questions?	Yes, I do. / No, I don't think so.
	When can you start?	Right away. / On Monday. / Next week.
	I'll be in touch.	I look forward to hearing from you.

C 🔄 Imagine that you're applying for the blogger job from **A**. Add two more skills or adjectives to the job description and create a new dialog with a partner. Use the Useful Expressions to help you.

D 👥 Perform your conversation for another pair.

5 GRAMMAR

A Turn to page 210. Complete the exercises. Then do **B–E** below.

The Present Perfect Tense	
Question	**Response**
How long **have** you **worked** there? How long **has** she **worked** there?	(I**'ve worked** there) <u>for</u> two years. (She**'s worked** there) <u>since</u> 2012.

Use *for* + a length of time (*for ten minutes, for the summer, for two years, for a while, for a long time, for my whole life*).

Use *since* + a point in time (*since 2014, since last September, since Friday, since I was a child*).

B 🔊 **Pronunciation: Reduced *for* in time expressions.** Say the first question and answer in the grammar chart above. Then listen and repeat. **CD 2 Track 20**

C 🔊 🔁 **Pronunciation: Reduced *for* in time expressions.** Listen and complete the sentences with a time expression. Then practice saying them with a partner. **CD 2 Track 21**

1. I've lived in the same city for _____.

2. He hasn't been in class for _____.

3. I haven't eaten for _____.

D Write questions in the present perfect with *how long*.

1. go to this school   *How long have you gone to this school?* _____

2. study English   _____

3. know your best friend   _____

4. have the same hairstyle   _____

5. live in your current home   _____

E 👥 Use the questions in **D** to interview three of your classmates. Write their answers in the chart. Who has done each thing the longest? Share your results with the class.

Name	Question 1	Question 2	Question 3	Question 4	Question 5

6 COMMUNICATION

A Read the qualities, abilities, and experience below. On a separate piece of paper, list the qualities, abilities, and experience needed for these jobs: *video-game tester*, *camp counselor*, *lifeguard*, *dog walker*. You can use the ideas in the box more than once. Add your own ideas, too.

Qualities	Abilities / Experience	
• a personable and energetic person who loves the outdoors • an efficient person who is knowledgeable about computers • flexible, patient, and kind to animals • an adventurous and responsible person	**be able to...** • swim well • work flexible hours • walk long distances • work independently • speak English well	**have experience...** • caring for animals • working with children • playing video games

a lifeguard

B 🔁 Choose a job in **A** to apply for. Tell your partner your choice. Then:

- Complete the questions according to the job that your partner is applying for. Then use them to interview your partner. Take turns.

- After the interview, decide if your partner is good for the job. Why or why not?

> Thanks for coming in today.
> So, tell me... what do you
> do now?

Interview questions

Name: _____

Job he or she is applying for: _____

1. What do you do now? How long have you done it?

2. Are you _____? Give me an example.
   (quality)

3. Do you have any experience _____?
   (doing something)

4. Can you _____? Please explain.
   (ability)

5. Your question: _____?

LESSON B DREAM JOBS

I'm a crab fisherman in Alaska. It's a physically demanding job. I move cages that weigh over 50 kilos (110 pounds), often in terrible weather. It's also one of the most hazardous jobs in the world: a lot of people die doing it. But it's well paid: I can make $50,000 in eight weeks.

A lot of people think being a model is glamorous, but it can be exhausting (you work long hours) and dull (you wait for hours to be photographed). But it can be rewarding, too, especially if your picture is in a magazine.

1 VOCABULARY

A 🔁 Read about the jobs. Then answer the questions with a partner.

1. Look at the words in **blue**. Which have a positive meaning? Which have a negative meaning?

2. What are the advantages and disadvantages of each job?

B 🔁 Think of a different job for each adjective below. Which would you like to do? Which would you never do? Tell your partner.

dull: _____maçante_____

exhausting: _____

glamorous: _____

hazardous: ___perigoso___

demanding: ___exigente___

dead-end: _profissão sem futuro/não há para onde ir._

rewarding: _____

Word Bank
demanding ↔ easy I 2
dull / boring ↔ glamorous / exciting
exhausting / tiring ↔ relaxing tired
hazardous / dangerous ↔ safe
rewarding / pleasing ↔ unsatisfying
well-paid ↔ dead-end

130 UNIT 9 ● Work

2 LISTENING

A 🔄 **Make predictions.** Look at the photo. Gino is a storyboard artist. What do you think he does? Tell a partner.

B 🔊 **Check predictions.** Listen and choose the correct answer. **CD 2 Track 22**

a. He illustrates comic books.

b. He draws pictures for children's books.

c. He draws pictures of events in a movie.

d. He takes photos of famous actors.

C 🔊 **Listen for details.** Read the sentences. Then listen and circle *True* or *False*. Correct the false sentences. **CD 2 Track 23**

Gino thinks...

1. the best part of his job is meeting famous people.	True	False
2. his job is dull sometimes.	True	False
3. working with a director is usually pretty easy.	True	False
4. it's common to work long hours in his job.	True	False

D 🔊 **Take notes; Identify details.** Gino gives people advice about becoming a storyboard artist. Which advice does he give? Listen for key words and take some notes. Then choose the correct answers below. **CD 2 Track 24**

a. Be knowledgeable about making movies.

b. Be able to work independently.

c. Be a good artist.

d. Be a hard worker.

ℹ️ Notice how Gino uses the words *first*, *second*, and *finally* to list his points.

E 🔄 Does Gino's job sound interesting to you? Why or why not? Tell a partner.

3 READING

A 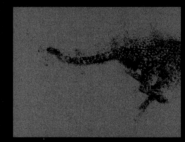 Find these words in your dictionary: *job, career, profession*. How are they similar? How is a *career* or *profession* different from a *job*? Tell a partner.

B 🔁 **Make predictions.** Read the title of the article and look at the images. Guess: What does a creative conservationist do? Tell a partner. Then read paragraph 1 to check your ideas.

C **Identify main ideas.** Read the article. In which paragraph (1–6) can you find the answer to each question below? Write the paragraph number next to the question.

_____ Is Asher's job ever dangerous? If so, how?

_____ When did Asher first become interested in animals?

_____ What's a typical day like for Asher?

_____ What caused Asher to make conservation her full-time job?

D 🔁 **Scan for details.** Check your answers in **C** with a partner. Then take turns asking and answering the four questions.

E **Scan for details; Infer information.** What personal qualities does Asher Jay have that make her good at her job? Underline ideas in the reading. Then think of two words not in the reading.

F 🔁 Answer the question at the end of the last paragraph of the passage. Your partner will suggest one possible job that matches your interests.

> I love to play the guitar. I also like to play video games.

> Maybe you could write music for video games.

ASHER JAY: CREATIVE CONSERVATIONIST

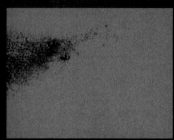

One of Asher Jay's paintings is of a cheetah. This animal's habitat (the land where it lives) is in danger.

A *conservationist* is a person who works to protect the environment.

1. Can your passion also be your profession? For "creative conservationist" Asher Jay, the answer is yes. She is an artist, writer, and activist. She uses her art to tell people about issues that affect animals around the world, like the illegal ivory trade and habitat loss.

2. Asher was born in India and was raised around the world to be a global citizen. She now lives in New York. She has been passionate[1] about wildlife since she was a child. As a girl, she often found sick animals and brought them home and cared for them. Her mother taught her that all life has a right to exist.

3. After learning about the BP oil spill[2] in 2010, Asher decided that caring for her planet was no longer a choice. She could no longer doubt her passion for wildlife. "I think that was when I realized this was more than a profession. It was my purpose on this planet!" she says. "I love animals, and when you care about something, it becomes your… responsibility to protect it for future generations."

4. Asher loves what she does, but working with nature can still result in unexpected and hazardous experiences. One night, while she was in Africa for work, she woke up and heard lions walking around her tent. Asher was scared, but the experience was still rewarding. "Nature is a… tutor," she says, "and the learning never stops."

5. On a typical day, Asher spends a lot of time working on her art, which includes paintings, billboards, films, and sculptures. But anything can happen, and each day is unpredictable, so Asher has to be flexible. "I never know what's next for me," she explains.

6. Asher Jay has turned her love for art and animals into a job. She says there are many ways to turn what you care about into a career. So, what are *you* passionate about?

[1] A *passion* is something you love or feel strongly about. If you are *passionate* about something, you care about it a lot.
[2] If there is an *oil spill*, oil comes out of a ship and goes into the water.

4 GRAMMAR

A Turn to page 211. Complete the exercises. Then do **B** and **C** below.

Verb + Infinitive	
I **like** <u>to sing</u>. I **want** <u>to be</u> a singer. She **needed** <u>to move</u> to London for work.	Certain **verbs** can be followed by an <u>infinitive</u> (*to* + verb): *agree, arrange, attempt, choose, decide, expect, forget, hate, hope, learn, like, love, need, plan, prepare, start, try, want.*

B Work in a small group. Look at the list of jobs below. Add two more ideas to the list.

taxi driver	film director	fashion designer
flight attendant	ski instructor	_____
police officer	astronaut	_____

C Follow the steps below to play this game with your group.

1. Student A begins. Choose a job from **B**. Don't tell your group the job.

2. Using a verb from the box, the other students take turns asking one question each to discover Student A's job.

try	choose	want	learn	need	plan	hate	like	hope	love

3. Student A answers the questions. Then together, the other students get one guess about Student A's job.

4. Then the next student goes. Repeat steps 1–3.

> How did you learn to do your job?

> I taught myself.

> In the job, do you need to wear special clothes?

5 WRITING

A Read the note about Career Day and look at the presentation slides on the next page. Then answer the questions with a partner.

1. Have you ever been to a Career Day at school or another place?

2. Have you ever used visual support (slides, video, or photos) in a presentation?

> **i** In the United States, Career Day is a day when students learn about different jobs. Students might give presentations, or people who do certain jobs might come to school to talk about their careers.

1.

SO YOU WANT TO BE A CHEF?

3.

The Disadvantages

1. **It's demanding.**

   You work long hours, often six or seven days a week.

2. **It's not well paid.**

   According to* *Chef Career Magazine*, an assistant chef only makes $20,000 a year at first.

2.

The Advantages

1. **There are many jobs.**

   Chefs work in restaurants, hotels, schools, cruise ships, and even on TV.

2. **It's rewarding.**

   It feels good to feed people good food.

3. **It's never dull.**

   Every day is busy and different.

4.

The Requirements

You need to be...

1. **passionate** about food.

   You have to love to cook and be willing to try new things in the kitchen.

2. **energetic.**

   You're going to work LONG hours.

*If you use specific facts or quote something directly, name your source by using *according to*.

B A student has prepared a short Career Day presentation about a job. Read the slides in **A** and answer the questions with a partner.

1. What job is it?

2. What are the advantages and disadvantages of this job?

3. What training, skills, or personal qualities do you need for the job?

C Choose a job and prepare a short slide show presentation about it. Use the example in **A** as a model, and answer questions 1–3 in **B**. Your goal is to teach others about this job.

6 COMMUNICATION

A Work in a group. Take turns giving your presentation from Writing **C**. When you listen, answer questions 1–3 from Writing **B** about your group members' jobs.

> Today, I'm going to talk to you about being a chef. There are good and bad things about this job. Let's talk about the advantages first...

B At the end, tell your group: Which of your group members' jobs would you like to do? Which would you hate to do? Why?

> I don't like to cook, so I'd hate to be a chef. It would be unsatisfying to me...

1 STORYBOARD

A Harry is telling Linda about his dream. Complete the story. For some blanks, more than one answer is possible.

B Cover the story. Take turns telling it to your partner.

2 SEE IT AND SAY IT

A 🔄 Yesterday there was a movie premiere at the Galaxy Theater. Look at the picture. What were the people doing when the movie star arrived? Tell your partner.

B 🔄 Think of a movie you know. Write the name of the movie on the sign in the picture. Invite your partner to the premiere. Your partner should ask one or two questions.

> How'd you like to see the new *Batman* movie with me?

> Sure. When?

> After class.

> I'd love to, but...

C 🔄 Invite other friends to see the movie. Practice inviting and accepting or refusing invitations.

3 LISTENING

A 🔊 Read the information in the box. Then listen and complete each person's profile below. Use one word in each blank. **CD 2 Track 26**

> Every year, the Dream Big Foundation gives $10,000 to a person between the ages of 17 and 22 so that he or she can do something important—go to college, study abroad, start a business, and so on. This year, the foundation received thousands of applications from all over the world. There are now two finalists—Teresa Silva and Daniel Okoye. Who should get the prize?

Name: Teresa Silva   **Age:** 21

What she does:

- She created a ___wibsite___ to help poor artists sell their products to the _____.
- When a product sells, she takes _____ percent and gives _____ percent to the artists.
- Since _____, she has already sold _____ items.

Why she needs the money:

- There's a lot of _____ to do.

What she plans to do with the money:

- She plans to _____ one more person.
- She hopes to sell _____ as many items.

Name: Daniel Okoye   **Age:** 18

What he does:

- He's a ___student___.
- He's from ___nigia___, but he moved to ___londen___ when he was eleven.

Why he needs the money:

- His parents ___15___ when he was ___died___.
- He has no money for ___university___.

What he plans to do with the money:

- He wants to study ___medisin___.
- He hopes to become a ___doctor with det___ and help others.

B You work for the Dream Big Foundation. Review your notes in **A**. Answer the questions.

1. Which words in the box below would you use to describe Teresa and Daniel? Why?

2. In your opinion, which person should win the money? Why? Give at least two reasons.

courageous	cautious	clever	efficient	flexible
ambitious	careless	independent	pleasant	punctual

C 👥 Get into a group of three or four people. Compare your answers in **B**. Together choose the winner of this year's prize. Then share your answer with the class.

> I think Teresa should get the money because she's very clever.

> So do I.

> Yeah, but Daniel lost his parents as a teenager and...

4 SPOT THE ERRORS

A Find and correct the mistake(s) in the sentences. You have five minutes.

1. A: I really liked that movie.
    B: So am I.

2. After graduation, I hope visit my cousin in New York City.

3. Sorry I missed your call. I watched TV, and I didn't hear the phone.

4. You seem quietly today. Are you OK?

5. Maya's worked for the same company since two years. Now she wants quit and get a new job.

6. A: How long you know John?
    B: Since high school. We are friends for many years.

B Compare your answers in **A** with a partner's. If you have different answers, explain your corrections.

5 SPEAK FOR A MINUTE!

A Read the questions and think about your answers. Do not tell anyone your answers.

1. Talk about the last movie you saw. What was the story about?

2. Talk about a festival or holiday that you know. Where and when does it take place? What happens?

3. Which would you prefer to do—work for a company or work for yourself? Why?

4. Talk about the last party you went to. What was it for? Who hosted it? Did you have a good time? Why or why not?

5. To speak English well, what do you need to do? What should you try not to do?

6. Name something you've wanted to do for a long time. Why haven't you done it yet?

B Get into a group of four people. Follow the steps below.

1. On six small pieces of paper, write the numbers 1 to 6 (for questions 1–6 in **A**). Put the six numbers in a hat or bag.

2. One person picks a number out of the hat or bag and answers that question in **A**.

3. If the person can talk for one minute without stopping, he or she gets one point. Then put the number back in the bag.

4. Then it's another person's turn. Repeat steps 2 and 3. Continue playing for 20 minutes. The winner is the person with the most points.

10 TELEPHONING

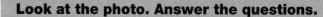

Look at the photo. Answer the questions.

1 What are these people doing?

2 Do you ever have to do this?

3 What kind of phone do you have now? Do you like it?

UNIT GOALS

1 Use formal and informal language on the phone

2 Talk about phone etiquette

3 Discuss plans and opinions

4 Describe your personal phone habits

In the country of Djibouti, migrants from Somalia search for a phone signal in order to call home.

1 VIDEO A Conference Call in Real Life

A  What are the challenges of holding a conference call with people in many different places? Discuss with a partner.

B ▶ Read about the challenges of conference calls below. Then watch and check off the ones you see in the video.

> ### Word Bank
>
> A *conference call* or *teleconference* is a telephone meeting for people in different locations. Each person *joins the meeting* by calling in on a separate phone, entering an *access code*, and saying their name.

The challenges of conference calls

☐ Some people are late in joining the call.

☐ The conversation can be awkward.

☐ The calls are too expensive.

☐ There are too many outside interruptions.

☐ People talk at the same time.

☐ No one leads the call.

☐ You can't hear well.

☐ Some people leave the call early.

C  Do you think conference calls are useful? Why or why not? Discuss with a partner.

2 VOCABULARY

Word Bank
Phrases with *phone*
answer the phone ↔ hang up the phone
turn on your phone ↔ turn off your phone
mute / silence your phone
be on the phone / talk on the phone
borrow / use someone's phone
Phrases with *call*
call someone / make a call
call someone back / return a call
get a call from someone
screen your calls
Phrases with *message*
get a (text / phone) message ↔
leave a message[1] / send a message[2]
check your (text / phone) messages
take a message

[1]You *leave* a (voice) message on the phone.   [2]You *send* text messages.

A   Look at the Word Bank. Use a dictionary to look up any words you don't know.

B   Use the Word Bank to complete the dialogs below. Use the correct form of the verb. In some cases, more than one answer may be possible.

1.   A: Emily just called. She's running five minutes late.

     B: Really? But the movie is starting in five minutes!

     A: Let's _____ her a text message. Now, what should we tell her?

2.   A: Hello, is Mr. Choi there?

     B: He is, but he's _____ the phone right now.

     A: Oh, OK. Can I _____ a message for him?

3.   A: Your phone is ringing. Are you going to _____ it?

     B: No, I'm not. I'm _____ my calls.

     A: I see. Who are you trying to avoid?

4.   A: Can I _____ your phone for a second?

     B: Sure. Here you go.

     A: Thanks. I have to _____ a couple of calls right away.

5.   A: Your phone is beeping. I think you need to _____ your text messages.

     B: You're right. Wow! I just _____ 13 new messages!

     A: Really? Who are they from?

C   Work with a partner. Choose one of the dialogs in **B**. Add two more lines to it. Then perform your dialog for another pair.

A 🔊 **Pronunciation: Stress in clarification questions.** Listen to the dialog. Notice the intonation of B's sentence. Why does B stress the underlined number? **CD 2 Track 27**

A: My number is 555-6749.

B: 555-6749?

A: Yes. 6-7-4-9.

B 🔊 **Pronunciation: Stress in clarification questions.** Listen and complete the dialogs. **CD 2 Track 28**

1. A: My Skype username is nancy_p12.

   B: Did you say _____?

   A: No, p12. That's p as in *Paul*.

2. A: My username is @photoguy.

   B: _____?

   A: That's correct.

3. A: My email address is joym@sf.edu.

   B: Was that _____ at sf.edu?

   A: No, it's joy m as in *Mary*.

Many people use Skype to communicate with friends, family, and coworkers around the world.

ℹ How to say these symbols:
@ = at
_ = underscore
# = hashtag

C 🔄 Practice the dialogs in **B** with a partner. Then use your own information and practice again.

D 🔊 **Make predictions; Infer information.** Read the sentences below. Then listen to six dialogs. In each dialog, what could be said next? Choose the best response. **CD 2 Track 29**

1. a. OK, I'll check my messages.
   b. No, thanks. I'll call back later.
   c. Yes, I left a message.

2. a. Please leave me a message, and I'll call you back.
   b. Would you like to leave a message?
   c. May I ask who's calling?

3. a. When is a good time to call?
   b. OK, I'll return your call.
   c. Thanks, I will.

4. a. No, he sent me a text message.
   b. He can't come to class today.
   c. I don't know. He hung up.

5. a. Are you screening your calls?
   b. Check your text messages.
   c. Hang up and call me back.

6. a. You can make a call.
   b. Don't forget to silence your phone.
   c. Can I borrow your phone?

E 🔊 **Check predictions.** Listen and check your answers. **CD 2 Track 30**

F 🔄 What does the voicemail greeting on your cell phone say? Say it to a partner in English.

4 SPEAKING

A 🔊 Celia and Lisa are chatting when their phone call is interrupted. Listen to the conversations. Which one is more formal? **CD 2 Track 31**

LISA: Hello?

CELIA: Lisa? Hi. It's Celia.

LISA: Oh, hey, Celia. How are you doing?

CELIA: Pretty good. So, are you ready for the big test tomorrow?

LISA: Almost, but I have one question... (phone beeps) Oh, Celia... can you hang on? I've got another call coming in.

CELIA: Yeah, no problem.

LISA: Hello?

PROF. LARSON: Yes, hello. May I speak to Lisa Sanchez, please?

LISA: Speaking.

PROF. LARSON: Lisa, this is Professor Larson. You left me a message earlier today. You had a question about tomorrow's exam.

LISA: Oh, right. Professor Larson, could you hold for a moment?

PROF. LARSON: Of course.

LISA: Hello, Celia? Can I call you back? I have to take the other call.

CELIA: Sure. Talk to you later.

B 👥 Practice the conversation in **A** with two classmates. Use your own names in the conversation.

SPEAKING STRATEGY

C 🔁 Make the conversation below more formal by changing the underlined words. Use the Useful Expressions to help you. Then practice it with a partner.

A: Hello?

B: <u>Hi. Is Kurt there?</u> _____

A: <u>Who's calling?</u> _____

B: This is Martin.

A: OK, <u>hang on.</u> _____

B: Sure.

A: Sorry, he's not in.
   <u>Can I take a message?</u> _____

B: No, thanks. I'll call back later.

D 🔁 Create two phone conversations with your partner. One should be informal. The other should be more formal.

Useful Expressions	
Using the Telephone	
Asking for someone and responding	Hi, Lisa? / Hi. Is Lisa there?
	Hello. May / Could / Can I speak to Lisa, please? [formal]
	This is Lisa. / Speaking.
Asking for identification of caller	Who's calling?
	May I ask who's calling? [formal]
Asking someone to wait	Hang on. / Can you hang on (for a moment / second)?
	Would / Could you hold (for a moment / second)? [formal]
Taking a message	Can I take a message?
	May I take a message? [formal]
	Would you like to leave a message? [formal]

E 👥 Perform your conversations for another pair. Can they guess which one is more formal?

5 GRAMMAR

A Turn to page 212. Complete the exercises. Then do **B–D** below.

Asking for Permission						Responses
Would	it be OK	if	I	used	your phone?	Certainly. / Of course. / Sure, no problem. (I'm) sorry, but…
Would	you mind					No, not at all. / No, go ahead. (I'm) sorry, but…
Do	you mind	if	I	use	your phone?	No, not at all. / No, go ahead. (I'm) sorry, but…
May / **Could** / **Can**		I	use	your phone?		Certainly. / Of course. / Sure, no problem. (I'm) sorry, but…

B Look at the photo. The passenger is asking the flight attendant for permission. Use the words in parentheses to complete the questions.

1. (move to another seat)

   Would you _____?

2. (have a vegetarian meal)

   May _____?

3. (use the restroom now)

   Would it _____?

4. (turn on my laptop now)

   Can _____?

C Read each situation. Use the verbs in parentheses to ask permission.

1. Your friend is doing his or her homework. You have finished your homework, and you want to watch TV. Ask permission informally. (turn on)

   _____

2. You're invited to a party on Saturday night. You want your friend to go, too. Ask the host's permission a little formally. (bring)

   _____

3. You were sick yesterday and missed an important test in class. You want to take it this Friday. Ask your instructor's permission formally. (take)

   _____

4. Your instructor doesn't allow phones in class. You are waiting for an important text and need to leave your phone on silent. Ask your instructor's permission formally. (check)

   _____

D 🔁 With a partner, take turns asking and answering the questions in **C**. Refuse (say *no* to) one request and give a reason why.

6 COMMUNICATION

A 👥 Get into groups of three: Student A, Student B, and Student C. Read the instructions.

Student A: Choose one piece of good news from the list below.

☐ I bought a new car! ☐ I got an "A" on my exam! ☐ I've got two tickets to a concert!

☐ I found your lost wallet! ☐ I got a new job! ☐ your idea: _____

Student B: Have a piece of paper and a pen ready to write down a message.

Student C: Choose a reason you are busy from the list below.

☐ You're taking a nap. ☐ You're out with friends.

☐ You're at the library. ☐ your idea: _____

B 👥 Work with your group. Follow the steps below.

Step 1: Student A has some good news for Student C, but Student B answers the phone. Student B explains why Student C is busy and takes Student A's message.

   A: Hello. May I speak to Bianca, please?

   B: I'm sorry, she's taking a nap. Can I take a message?

   A: Yes. This is Ernesto. Would you tell her I found her wallet?

   B: Sure, no problem. What's your number?

   A: It's...

Step 2: Student B writes down the message and gives the information to Student C.

● :: WHILE YOU WERE OUT :: ●

Ernesto called.

Time: _3:30_

Message: _He found your wallet._

Phone number: _555-9733_

> **Remember! How to make a request**
>
> **Can / Could / Will / Would** you answer the phone?
>
> OK. / Sure, no problem. / I'd be glad to.
>
> **Would you mind** answering the phone?
>
> No, not at all. / No, I'd be glad to.

Step 3: Student C calls Student A back to find out about the good news. Ask at least two questions.

   C: Hi, Ernesto. It's Bianca.

   A: Hi, Bianca. I have some good news. I found your wallet.

   C: That's great! Where did you find it?

   A: In the school cafeteria.

   C: Thanks a lot, Ernesto. Could you bring it to school tomorrow?

C 👥 Switch roles so everyone gets a chance to play each role.

It is polite to step aside if you need to use your phone in a busy place.

1 VOCABULARY

A 📲 Read the quiz. Pay attention to the words in **blue**. Use your dictionary to help you. Talk about the meanings of the words with a partner. Then complete the chart with a word or phrase in **blue**.

Word	Opposite
add / post	delete
ban	*allow*
polite	*rude*
⌐ raise your voice	
respond	ignore
thoughtless	
turn down (the music)	
turn down (a request)	

> If you *respond* to a question, you answer it. The opposite is *ignore*.

B Take the quiz. Check (✓) your answers.

C 📲 Explain your answers in **B** to a partner.

Phone Etiquette: How polite are you?

1. You're on a date. You get a text from a friend. What do you do?
   - ☐ Check it and **respond** right away.
   - ☐ **Ignore** the message. Answering it now would be **rude**.
   - ☐ My idea: _____

2. The person next to you on the bus is listening to loud music. What do you do?
   - ☐ Ask him to **turn down** the music. You don't want to hear it!
   - ☐ Put on your headphones and **turn up** your music loud, too.
   - ☐ My idea: _____

3. I think we should...
   - ☐ **ban** phones in crowded places like subways and airplanes. No one should be able to use them.
   - ☐ **allow** phones everywhere. I should always be able to use my phone.
   - ☐ My idea: _____

4. When talking on my phone in public, I usually...
   - ☐ **raise my voice** so the caller can hear me clearly.
   - ☐ **lower my voice**. I don't want others to hear my conversation.
   - ☐ My idea: _____

5. You want to post some funny photos of your friend online, but the photos might be embarrassing. What do you do?
   - ☐ Show your friend the photos first. It's the **thoughtful** thing to do.
   - ☐ Post the photos. If he doesn't like them, you can **delete** them.
   - ☐ My idea: _____

6. You just started a new job, and your boss sends you a friend request on social media. What do you do?
   - ☐ **Accept** the request. He must like me!
   - ☐ **Turn down** the request. I don't want people at work seeing my personal information.
   - ☐ My idea: _____

2 LISTENING

A 🔊 **Listen for gist.** Read the sentences below. Then listen to three different conversations and choose the best answer for each sentence. **CD 2 Track 32**

Word Bank

If a person does something *at the last minute*, he or she does it at the latest time possible.

Conversation 1

1. The speakers are in a _____.

   a. classroom   b. restaurant   c. movie theater

Conversation 2

2. The speakers are _____ a party.

   a. taking photos at   b. posting pictures from   c. looking at photos from

Conversation 3

3. The speakers are waiting for their friend Manny. Manny is _____.

   a. late for a party   b. still at school   c. talking on his phone

B 🔊 **Listen for details; Infer information.** Listen again and choose the best answer. **CD 2 Track 32**

Conversation 1

1. The man is asking the girl to _____.

   a. turn off her phone   b. lower her voice   c. turn down her music

2. The girl _____.

   a. apologizes and agrees   b. ignores the man   c. gets angry with the man

Conversation 2

3. The girl thinks the photo of her is _____.

   a. thoughtful   b. silly   c. terrible

4. The girl decides to _____.

   a. ignore people's comments   b. tell Connor to delete the photos   c. both a and b

Conversation 3

5. The guy texts Manny, and Manny _____.

   a. responds right away   b. ignores the text   c. calls the guy

6. The girl thinks Manny is _____.

   a. polite   b. angry   c. thoughtless

C 🔄 Answer the questions with a partner.

1. In each conversation, what happened? Use your answers in **A** and **B** to help you explain.

2. Have any of these things ever happened to you?

> In the first conversation, the girl was... and the man asked her to...

3 READING

PHONE-FREE
ON THE ROAD?

A 🔄 **Read for the gist.** Read the title and first paragraph on the next page. Tell a partner: What does the new law do?

B **Read for opinions.** Read the article. Then complete the sentences below. Why does each person have this opinion about cell phones and driving? Write a reason.

1. Simon thinks some / all cell phone use should be allowed / banned.
Reason: _____
_____

2. Alexis thinks some / all cell phone use should be allowed / banned.
Reason: _____
_____

3. Ann thinks some / all cell phone use should be allowed / banned.
Reason: _____
_____

C **Infer meaning.** Find these expressions in the reading:

come on, I mean, look

Match each expression with its meaning.

Use this expression to…

1. say you disagree with something
_____

2. make something you've just said clearer _____

3. introduce an important point
_____

D 👥 **Summarize and evaluate; Exemplify.** Work in a group of three. Follow the steps below.

1. Each person should take one person's comment and read it aloud. Try to read with feeling.

2. Role-play a conversation among the three people. Talk about the law and your opinion about it. Try to make the others agree with you.

3. Whose opinion(s) from the reading do you agree with? Why?

A new law bans all cell phone use while you are driving—including talking on the phone and texting. The fine[1] for breaking the law[2] is high, but many drivers are ignoring the ban. What do you think about this problem?

Simon R. Peru

disagree

<u>Look</u>, I've got a phone, and I'm glad to have it. But <u>come on</u>! Talking on the phone, checking social media, or texting while you're driving is crazy. And yet, I see people doing things like this every day. Using your phone and driving at the same time causes accidents. There have been many studies to prove this. My question is, where are the police? They don't seem to care, so it's easy for drivers to ignore the law. When people are afraid of getting a large fine, phone use in the car will stop. Everyone needs to learn that when you drive, you should turn off your phone. It's very simple!

Alexis C. Greece

Ok, I agree—texting while driving is hazardous. But can we really ban all phone use in cars? For example, yesterday I was driving home, and I saw an accident on the road. I called and reported it. Did I stop driving to make the call? No. But did I help someone? Yes. We need to talk more about this new law. I just don't think the answer to the problem is so simple.

Ann T. China

I don't think we can ban all phone use in cars—especially if you use a hands-free device[3] while driving, like I do. Sometimes my friend is in the car with me. I talk to her while I'm driving. Isn't that dangerous? <u>I mean</u>, isn't talking on the phone the same as talking to a passenger? In my opinion, they are the same, and so I think we should be able to chat on the phone while we're driving.

[1]A *fine* is money you pay when you break a law.

[2]If you *break a law*, you do something illegal.

[3]A *hands-free device* allows you to use your phone in the car without touching it or looking at it.

4 GRAMMAR

A Turn to page 213. Complete the exercises. Then do **B** and **C** below.

Verb + Infinitive vs. Verb + Gerund	
I **need** <u>to buy</u> a new phone.	Certain verbs can be followed by an <u>infinitive</u>: *agree, decide, hope, learn, need, plan, seem, want, would like*
I **avoid** <u>talking</u> on the phone when I'm driving.	Certain verbs can be followed by a <u>gerund</u>: *appreciate, avoid, dislike, enjoy, feel like, keep*
I **tried** <u>to call</u> / <u>calling</u> you earlier.	Certain verbs can be followed by an infinitive or a gerund: *begin, can't stand, hate, like, love, prefer, start, try*

B How do you feel about the activities below? Write sentences in your notebook, using the verbs in the box.

avoid	can't stand / hate	enjoy	like	(not) mind	need	prefer

Example: I hate talking on the phone. I prefer to text people.

1. talk on the phone
2. respond to texts late at night
3. walk and text at the same time
4. take selfies in public

5. post weird photos of myself online
6. say mean things on social media
7. play games on my phone
8. accept friend requests from strangers online

C 👥 Work in a small group. Compare your answers in **B**.

> I can't stand when people take selfies in public.

> Really? I think it's fun.

5 WRITING

A Read the question and the paragraph. Then discuss with a partner: What is the writer's response? What examples does she give to explain her response?

B List all the ways you use your phone in a day. Then use your notes and the example to write a paragraph that answers the question. Use at least two verbs from the grammar chart.

C Exchange papers with a partner.

1. Answer the questions in the direction line in **A**. Circle any mistakes in your partner's paper.

2. Return the paper to your partner. Make corrections to your own paragraph.

3. Are you and your partner similar or different? Why do you think people spend so much time on their phones?

Question: *Do you spend a lot of time on your phone? Why or why not?*

Yes, I spend a lot of time on my phone. For example, when I wake up, I check my phone and I respond to texts right away. Then I check social media. When I have breakfast, I can't stand just eating. I prefer to watch a video or play a game. Even at the bus stop, I dislike just waiting. I usually call a friend or browse the Internet. At night, I avoid doing my homework by using my phone. I text my friends or listen to music. My mom tried to ban phones from 7:00 to 10:00 PM in our house, but it didn't work. We are all addicted to our phones!

6 COMMUNICATION

A Work in a group of four. Felipe is 11 years old. He wants a phone. Each group member should choose one person below. Read <u>only</u> the information for your part.

Word Bank
If you are *addicted* to something, you can't stop doing it.

Felipe Dias

I want to get a phone. All my friends have one. I need one to text my friends, watch videos, and play games. And without a phone, I don't know what my friends are doing.

Mrs. Dias

I don't mind getting Felipe a phone. He has so many after-school activities, and I worry about him. I can't stand wondering where he is. I want to be able to text or call him if I have to.

Mr. Dias

I've avoided getting Felipe a phone. I know he wants one, but I'd prefer to wait another year. Do you know how many adults are addicted to their phones? I mean, at his age, Felipe should be playing sports, not staring at a screen.

Felipe's school principal

Cell phones are convenient, but too much phone use can be bad for children's brains. Also, there are lots of problems these days with Internet bullying at school, and phones make this easy. Texting in class is also a problem. I don't think kids should bring phones to school.

B Role-play a discussion among the four people. Each person should explain his or her opinion. Bring in your own ideas, too. Try to make the other people agree with you.

C Should Felipe get a phone? Why or why not? What is your group's final decision? Tell the class.

Come on, Dad. I need a phone. All my friends have one!

Look, Felipe, you don't need to have a cell phone.

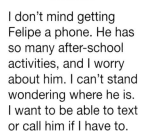

*In my opinion I
I m agree with Dias*

11 TECHNOLOGY

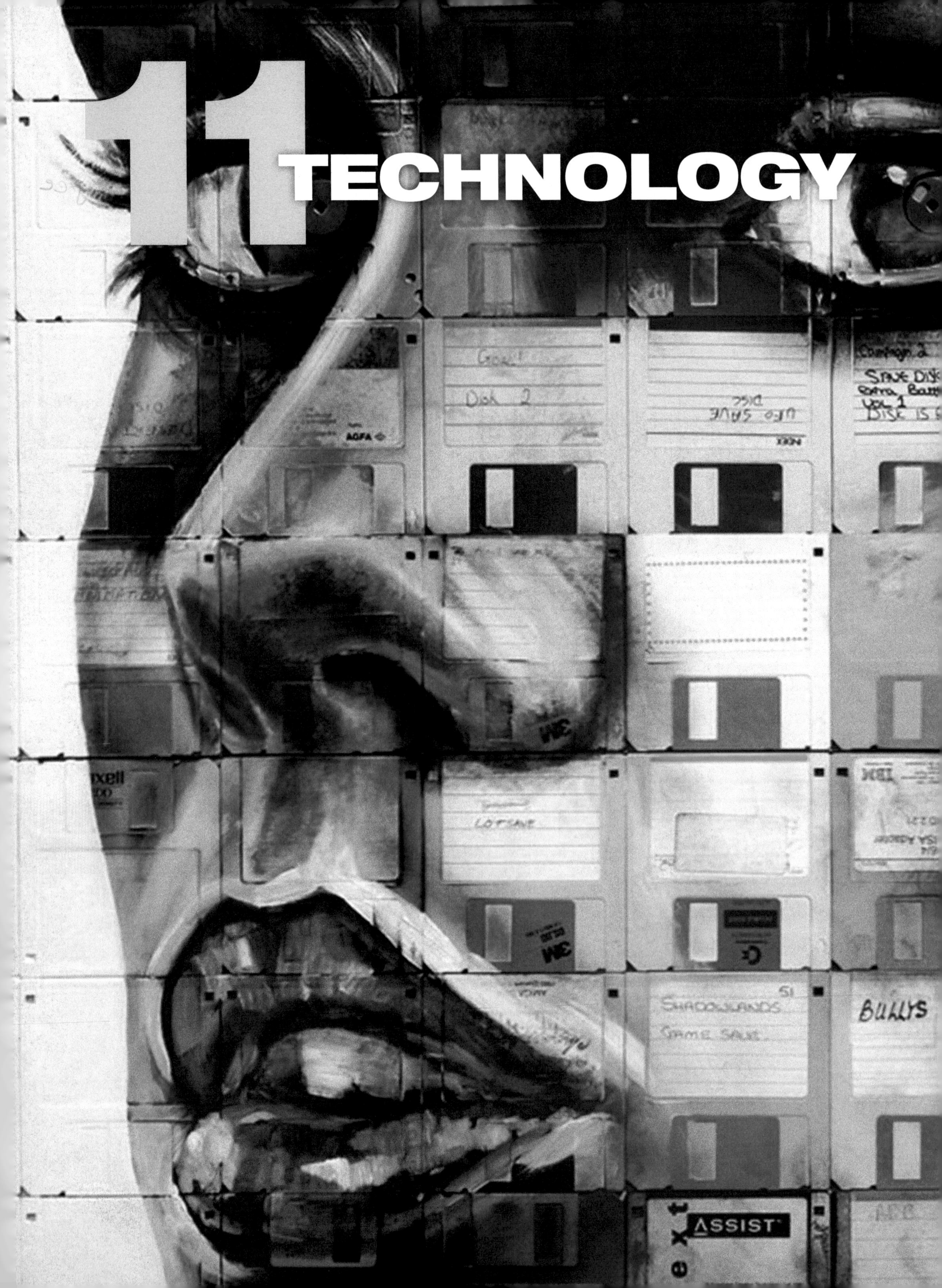

Artist Nick Gentry uses old technology (such as these floppy disks) to create portraits.

Look at the photo. Answer the questions.

1 What old technology is in the picture?

2 Do you know what they were used for? Guess.

3 How has technology improved our lives in the last ten years? Name one way.

UNIT GOALS

1 Describe a gadget

2 Describe how things used to be

3 Talk about events in the past that no longer happen

4 Compare similar items

The Apple II personal computer came out in 1977. It was one of the first bestsellers in the computer industry.

1 **VIDEO** Kids React to Old Computers

A Look at the computer in the photo. How have computers changed since then? Think of one or two ways. Tell a partner.

B Look up any words you don't know. Then watch the video. Check (✓) the items you see.

☑ an error message   ☑ a monitor   ☐ a keyboard   ☐ a mouse

☑ an on switch   ☑ a screen   ☐ a printer

C Read the kids' statements below and try to guess the answers. Then watch the video again and check your answers.

button	desk	Internet	nothing	programs	televisions

1. Jayka: "If you don't have a _____desk_____, where do you put this?"

2. Tyler: "It's kind of like those old _____telev_____ that are very boxy."

3. Brooke-Monaé: "Apps! Games! Websites! Everything! But this thing right here has ___nothing___!"

4. Narrator: "You can't do anything, or even type until you hit a reset ___bottom___."

5. Dylan: "Are there any ___programs___ on it?"

6. Narrator: "How do you go on the ___internet___?"

D How did the kids feel about the old computer? How do you feel about it? Discuss with a partner.

2 VOCABULARY

Trying to get in shape? The BeFit makes your goals more **manageable** by tracking your exercise, activity patterns, and diet. This **remarkable** product tells time *and* helps you use your time well!

Product features

- It's **portable** and goes with you everywhere, so it gives you a **reliable** and complete picture of your daily activity.

- The BeFit is **dependable**: It performs perfectly even during your most intense workout!

- The BeFit comes in a variety of colors, so it is always **fashionable**.

Product reviews

Fitgurl2018 I started using a BeFit as a **practical** way to help me lose weight… I love it!

NotSoSure A lot of people are excited about this product, but it's not very **affordable**. It's too much money!

SaveYour$$! This is not as **durable** as they say… I wore mine to the beach, and now it doesn't work! *with good quality*

> **i** Remember, the suffixes *–able / -ible / -ble* mean *capable of* or *can.* If something is *affordable*, you can afford it (it is not too expensive).

A Read the ad above. Pay attention to the words in **blue**. Check (✓) True or False.

If something is…	True	False		If something is…	True	False
1. *affordable*, it's expensive.	☐	☑	5. *durable*, it breaks easily.	☐	☑
2. *remarkable*, it's not special.	☐	☑	6. *portable*, you can carry it easily.	☑	☐
3. *practical*, it's useful and logical.	☑	☐	7. *reliable*, you can trust it.	☑	☐
4. *manageable*, it's difficult to control.	☐	☑	8. *fashionable*, it is in style.	☑	☐

B 🔁 Check your answers in **A** with a partner. For the false statements, write correct definitions.

C 🔁 Answer the questions with a partner.

> I think my phone is really practical. I can do a lot of things on it.

1. What do you like about the BeFit?

2. Would you ever use a product like this? Why or why not?

3. Think of a gadget you own. Which words in blue from **A** would you use to describe it?

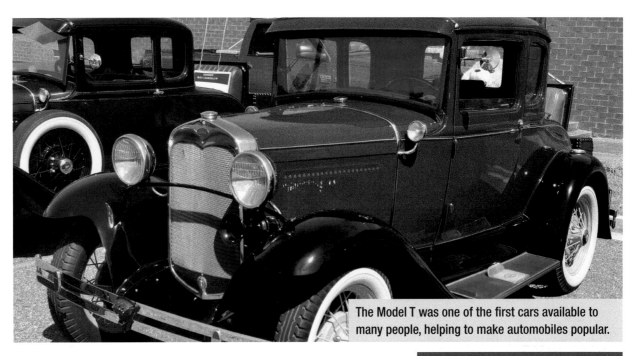

The Model T was one of the first cars available to many people, helping to make automobiles popular.

A Look at the words in the Word Bank. What do they mean? What is one recent fad? Tell a partner.

Word Bank

a fad = something popular for a short time

a flash in the pan = something successful for a short time

B **Listen for the main idea.** You are going to hear a lecture. Listen and choose the best title for the lecture. **CD 2 Track 34**

Guessing the Future: Predictions about technology that were _____.

a. remarkable   c. wrong

b. creative   d. confusing

C **Listen for details; Note taking.** Listen to the full lecture. Complete the missing information in the chart. **CD 2 Track 35**

Word Bank

one billion = 1,000,000,000

Year	Device	Prediction (then)	Description (now)	Number
1876	telephone	__american__ the telephone, but we do not.	indispensable ضروري	
1948	automobile	The __horse__ is here to stay, but the automobile is a __fad__.	convenient reliable	more than __one__ billion cars
	television	Television won't __last__. It's just a __flash__ in the __pan__.	affordable	around __1.4__ billion TVs
1995	Internet	The Internet will __fail__.		over __3__ billion users

D Choose one of the devices from **C** and predict how it will be different 20 years from now and 50 years from now. Tell a partner. Do you agree with his or her predictions? Why or why not?

4 SPEAKING

A 🔊 🔁 Listen to Alan and Kim's conversation. Then answer the questions with a partner. **CD 2 Track 36**

1. How would most people describe Kim's sister?

2. What is Kim's sister really like?

ALAN: Hey, Kim. I saw your sister on Facebook the other day. She's really changed a lot.

KIM: Yeah? Why do you say that? She still looks the same.

ALAN: Yeah, but now she's got all these friends, and she's really funny. She used to be so different—you know, kind of shy.

KIM: A lot of people say that about my sister. They think that she's this quiet person, but, actually, she's very outgoing.

ALAN: Really?

KIM: Yep. Once she feels comfortable with you, she's really friendly, and she talks a lot.

ALAN: Wow, I had no idea.

B 🔁 Practice the conversation with a partner. Do you know anyone like Kim's sister?

SPEAKING STRATEGY

Useful Expressions: Offering a Counterargument		
Stating what other people think	A lot of people say (that)...	she's really shy.
	Some people think (that)...	
Explaining what you think	(But,) actually,...	she's very outgoing.
	(But,) in fact, / in reality,...	
	(But,) the truth / fact / reality is...	

C Read the statements below and check (✓) the ones you agree with.

☐ Learning English is easy.

☐ Modern technology is always reliable.

☐ Everybody should get married someday.

☐ Wearing black is always fashionable.

☐ Activity trackers, such as the BeFit, are affordable.

☐ The apps on your phone should be practical.

D 🔁 With a partner, compare your opinions about the statements in **C**. Talk about the statements you <u>don't</u> agree with. Use the Useful Expressions to help you.

> Some people say learning English is easy, but, actually, it's hard.

E 🔁 Tell a partner something surprising about you or your country.

> A lot of people think it's warm in Spain all year, but, in reality, it's very cold in the winter.

> Why do you say that?

> Well, for one thing, there's the grammar. It's complex and...

5 GRAMMAR

A Turn to page 214. Complete the exercises. Then do **B–E** below.

Used to			
Subject	**use(d) to**	**Verb**	
I	**used to**	wear	glasses.
She	didn't **use to**	own	a computer.

Did	**Subject**	*use to*	**Verb**		**Responses**
Did	you	**use to**	wear	glasses?	Yes, I did. / No, I didn't.
	she		own	a computer?	Yes, she did. / No, she didn't.

B 🔊 Pronunciation: *Used to.* Listen to the sentences. Notice the different pronunciation of the *s* in *used / use to* and the *s* in the verb forms *use / used*. **CD 2 Track 37**

used / use to: s = /s/   use / used: s = /z/

1. People <u>used</u> to go to movie theaters a lot more.   3. What kind of computer do you <u>use</u>?

2. I didn't <u>use</u> to shop online.   4. I <u>used</u> my brother's cell phone.

C 🔊 🔄 Pronunciation: *Used to.* Listen to how the words *use* and *used* are pronounced. Check (✓) /s/ or /z/. Then take turns reading the sentences aloud with a partner. **CD 2 Track 38**

	/s/	/z/			/s/	/z/
1. She used the phone in her office.	☐	☐	3. Do you use a tablet?		☐	☐
2. My email used to be more manageable.	☐	☐	4. I didn't use to eat meat.		☐	☐

D 🔄 Unscramble the sentences. Then ask and answer the questions with a partner.

1. use to / you / somewhere else / did / live _____?

2. go / you / use to / to a different school / did _____?

3. use / did / use to / pay phones / people _____?

4. did / have / you / long hair / use to _____?

5. wear / did / use to / you / a watch _____?

E 👥 Follow the steps below.

1. Write down three true statements on three pieces of paper about things you used to do.

2. Give the papers to your instructor.

3. Your instructor will give you three pieces of paper with statements from your classmates.

4. Walk around the class and ask questions to find out who the papers belong to.

> Did you use to ride your bike to school everyday?

> Yes, I did, but it took forever! Now I take the bus to school.

6 COMMUNICATION

A 🔁 Three years ago, Tetsuya and his family moved from Tokyo to Los Angeles. Look at his old Tokyo profile (on the left) and his new Los Angeles profile (on the right). How has his life changed? With a partner, make sentences with *used to* and *didn't use to*.

> People used to call him Tetsuya. Now everyone calls him...

Three years ago

Tetsuya
Tokyo

About

My name is Tetsuya.

I live in Tokyo with my parents.

I wear a uniform to school.

I ride my bicycle to school.

I don't belong to any clubs at school.

I don't have many chances to practice my English.

Today

Ted
Los Angeles

About

Everyone here calls me "Ted."

I live in an apartment in L.A. with two roommates.

It's warm here. I wear a T-shirt almost every day!

I have a car! I drive to college.

I'm a member of the swim team.

I speak English all the time.

B Make notes about your life five years ago and now. Try to write down things that are different, if possible.

Five years ago	Now
Home: _____	Home: _____
Family: _____	Family: _____
Friends: _____	Friends: _____
Work / school: _____	Work / school: _____
Favorite activities: _____	Favorite activities: _____
Favorite TV shows / movies: _____	Favorite TV shows / movies: _____
Other: _____	Other: _____

C 🔁 Tell your partner how your life has changed in the past five years. Whose life—yours or your partner's—has changed the most?

> I still live in the same apartment, but my family situation has changed.

> My older brother used to live at home, but now he's away at college.

> How so?

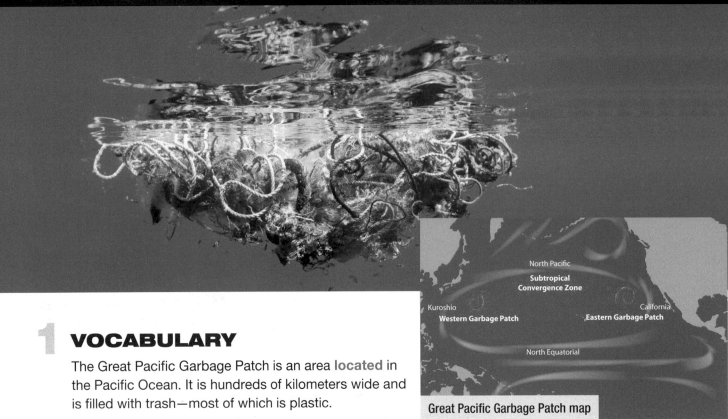

Great Pacific Garbage Patch map

1 VOCABULARY

The Great Pacific Garbage Patch is an area **located** in the Pacific Ocean. It is hundreds of kilometers wide and is filled with trash—most of which is plastic.

Eventually, this area may **have a negative effect** on humans. For example, fish that **consume** plastic because they think it is food won't be safe to eat.

Scientists are trying to **prevent** the growth of this area. They think we can prevent the growth of this area if we use less plastic and **recycle** any plastic we already have. They are also trying to **rescue** injured or sick animals in the area and use advanced technology to **transform** the plastic so that it breaks down faster. In time, this will **reduce** the amount of plastic in the area to almost nothing. Eventually, scientists hope to **restore** the area to its original state.

A Read the information. Then match a word or phrase in **blue** with its definition below.

نيبر

1. stop something from happening   _prevent_

2. decrease   _reduce_

3. save   _rescue_

4. reuse   _recycle_

5. eat or drink   _consume_
صرف در كردن

6. change something completely   _trenfoom_

7. have a bad influence   _have a nigative_

8. found in a certain place   _located_

9. make something like it was in the past   _restore._

B 🔁 Read the information in **A** again. Then with a partner, take turns answering these questions.

1. What and where is the Great Pacific Garbage Patch?

2. Why is this area a problem?

3. What are scientists doing about the problem?

4. In addition to recycling, how else can we reduce the amount of plastic we use?

2 LISTENING

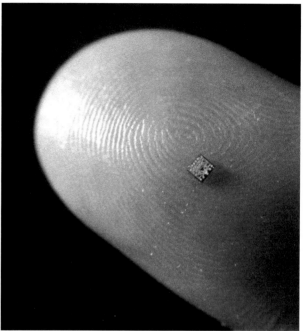

A Complete the sentences with the words *blind*, *sight*, and *vision*. Use your dictionary to help you.

1. _____ or _____ is the ability to see things.

2. If you are _____, you can't see.

B 🔊 **Listen for gist and details.** Look at the photos and read the sentences below. Then listen and choose the best answer to complete each one. **CD 2 Track 39**

1. The man is talking about a tool he and others are working on. This tool will ___*b*_____.

   a. prevent blindness from happening

   b. restore blind people's vision

   c. give blind people perfect vision

2. The glasses have a ___*C*_____ inside.

   a. computer chip   b. pen   c. video camera

e f f e c t **C** 🔊 **Listen to sequence events.** How does the tool work? Read the sentences below. Then listen again and put the steps in the order (1–5) they happen. **CD 2 Track 39**

___*4*___ The person can see the pen.

___*2*___ The blind person puts on special glasses and looks at an object, such as a pen.

___*5*___ The picture is sent to the chip in the person's eye.

___*1*___ Doctors put a computer chip in a blind person's eye.

___*3*___ The glasses take a picture of the pen.

D 🔄 Use your answers in **B** and **C** to explain how this new technology works. What do you think of this tool? Tell a partner.

A 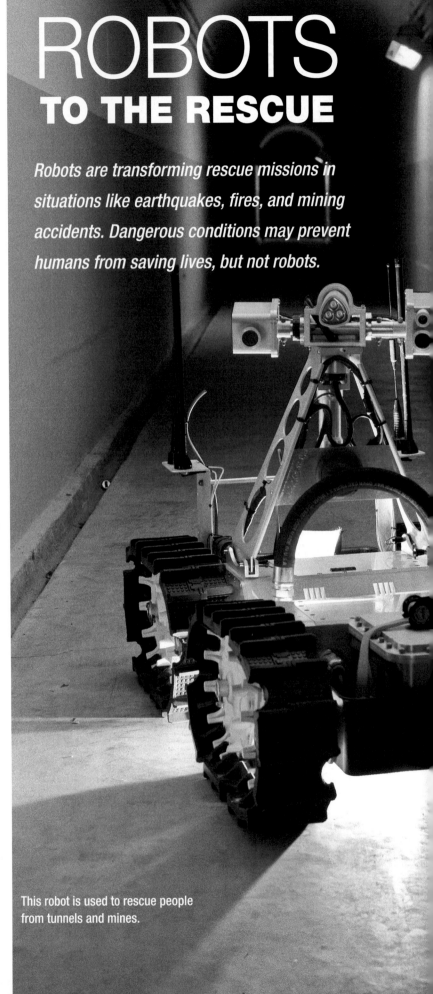 **Make predictions.** Read the title of the news article. Then look at the photo and read the caption. What do you think this article is about? Tell a partner. Then read the article to check your ideas.

B **Infer meaning.** Find the four underlined words in the passage and read the sentences they are in. Then match each word with its definition. One definition is extra.

1. collapsed _____
2. trapped _____
3. position _____
4. identified _____

a. discovered
b. put something down
c. fell down
d. unable to escape or move
e. location, place

C **Sequence events.** Morgan is telling people what happened. Number the events (1–9) in the order they happened.

_____ They took me to the hospital.

_____ Then the roof of the gym fell down, and I passed out.

_____ I went to the gym for my class.

_____ I have to stay for a couple of days, but I'm feeling much better!

_____ Then suddenly, this little robot appeared.

__1__ It was snowing really hard on Tuesday morning.

_____ A couple of men found me.

_____ When I woke up, I tried to move, but I couldn't. I was scared.

_____ I heard this really loud sound.

D 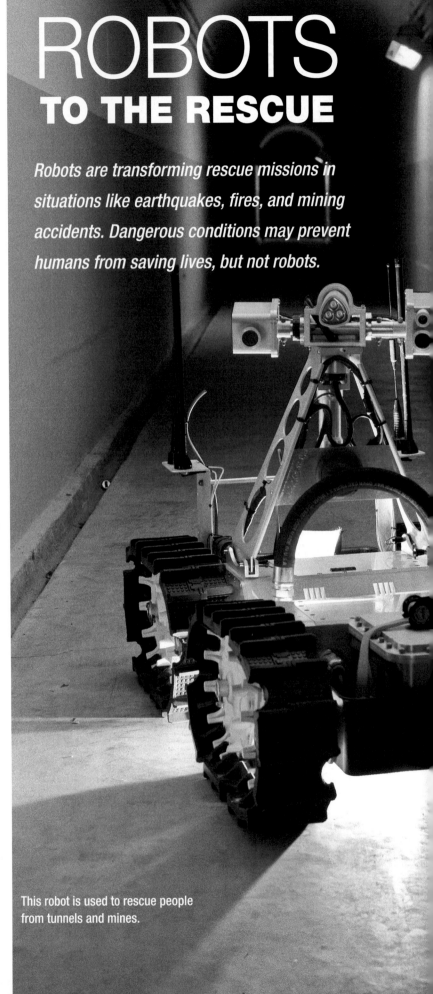 In what other kinds of situations could rescue robots be used? Tell a partner.

ROBOTS
TO THE RESCUE

Robots are transforming rescue missions in situations like earthquakes, fires, and mining accidents. Dangerous conditions may prevent humans from saving lives, but not robots.

This robot is used to rescue people from tunnels and mines.

1 She may have a broken leg, but she couldn't be happier. Morgan Bailey, 15, is lucky to be alive.

It seemed like a normal Tuesday for Morgan. She was at school. It was fourth period, and she was the first student to arrive in the
5 gymnasium for her physical education class.

Suddenly there was a loud noise.

"There was a sharp, cracking noise and then a loud boom. After that, I don't remember anything," said Morgan. "I guess I passed out.[1]"

10 The roof of the gymnasium had <u>collapsed</u> under the heavy snow. Morgan was <u>trapped</u> underneath. She couldn't escape.

"I woke up and there was a big piece of wood on my leg. I couldn't move it. I was starting to get cold."

Fortunately, help was nearby. A new program using rescue
15 robots was tried for the first time.

"We were nervous about using the robot," said Derrick Sneed, the man in charge of the program. "But in the end, the robot gave us reliable information. It went extremely well."

The rescue robot was able to go into the gym and locate
20 Morgan's exact <u>position</u>.

"We send in robots first because it's just more practical. A situation may not be safe for humans," said Mr. Sneed. A gas leak,[2] for example, could kill you or me, but wouldn't hurt a robot."

Although it didn't happen in Morgan's case, some rescue robots
25 can bring fresh air or water to people who are trapped.

"Once we <u>identified</u> Morgan's location and knew it was safe to go in, a couple of our men went in to <u>rescue</u> her," says Sneed. "Her leg was broken and she was scared, but thankfully, she was alive."

Doctors sent Morgan home from the hospital after only two
30 days. What's the first thing she wanted to do? "I wanted to meet my hero!" Morgan laughs. "That little robot saved my life!"

[1]If you *pass out*, you become unconscious.
[2]When a *gas leak* happens, the air is not safe to breathe.

4 GRAMMAR

A Turn to page 215. Complete the exercises. Then do **B** and **C** below.

Comparisons with *as... as*
Phone A is 12 centimeters. Phone B is 12 centimeters.
Phone A is **as** <u>big</u> **as** phone B.
Phone A costs $100. Phone B costs $100.
Phone A costs **as** <u>much</u> **as** phone B.

Camera A isn't **as** <u>affordable</u> **as** Camera B.
Maria didn't do **as** <u>well</u> **as** Carlos on the test.

B Read about the two cars. Then, with a partner, make sentences using *(not) as... as* about them. Which car do you think is better?

Both the Fiat and Tesla are electric cars.

	Car 1: Fiat 500e	Car 2: Tesla Model S
price	$32,000	$100,000+
durability	lasts 5+ years	lasts 5+ years
popularity	very popular	only with the rich

> They're both electric cars, but the Tesla isn't as affordable as the Fiat.

C With your partner, complete the chart with two more electronic devices (for example, two different phones, two different tablets). In your opinion, which product is better? Explain with sentences using *(not) as... as.*

	1: _____	2: _____
price		
size		
durability		
popularity		

5 WRITING

A 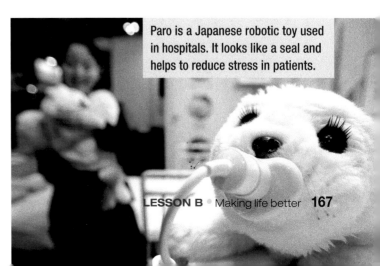 Read the paragraph. What two things is the writer comparing? Which one does she like more? Why? Tell a partner.

B Look at the two products you compared in Grammar **C**. Choose one and in a paragraph explain which product you think is better.

C Exchange papers with a partner.

1. Answer the questions in **A** about your partner's writing.

2. Circle any mistakes in your partner's writing. Then return the paper to your partner. Make changes to your own paper.

> I used to own a BeFit activity tracker, but two months ago, I got an iLife. Of the two activity trackers, I like the iLife better for a couple of reasons. First, the iLife lets me do a lot of things. I can track my activity. I can also see who is calling me, set alarms for myself, and many other things. The BeFit doesn't have as many features. Second, the BeFit uses a lot of power, so its battery doesn't last as long as the iLife's. For these two reasons, I think the iLife is a better product.

6 COMMUNICATION

A With a partner, design a robot that will do something useful for people. Discuss the questions below.

Name of our robot: _____

1. What is the purpose of the robot? Choose from the list below or write your own idea.

be a friend to children / adults	do household chores
work in schools	work in hospitals
do factory work / build things	your idea: _____

2. What exactly will the robot do?

3. What will the robot look like? Draw a simple picture on a separate piece of paper.

4. Why is the robot as good as (or better than) a human?

5. How much will the robot cost?

B Get together with another pair and take turns doing the following.

Presenters: Present your robot. Start by saying its name.

Listeners: As you listen to the other pair's presentation, answer questions 1–5 in **A**. At the end of the presentation, you may ask questions.

> Today, we're going to tell you about our robot, Robbie. He works in...

C Repeat **B** with two other pairs. At the end, compare notes with your partner and choose your favorite robot. Explain your choice to the class.

Paro is a Japanese robotic toy used in hospitals. It looks like a seal and helps to reduce stress in patients.

People watch the aurora borealis, or "northern lights," in Yellowknife, Canada.

Look at the photo. Answer the questions.

1 Where are these people? What are they looking at?

2 Would you go to this place on vacation?

3 Name a place that you want to visit. Why do you want to go there?

UNIT GOALS

1 Explain how you prepare for a trip

2 Say that something is necessary

3 Say that you forgot something

4 Ask and answer questions about what you have and haven't done

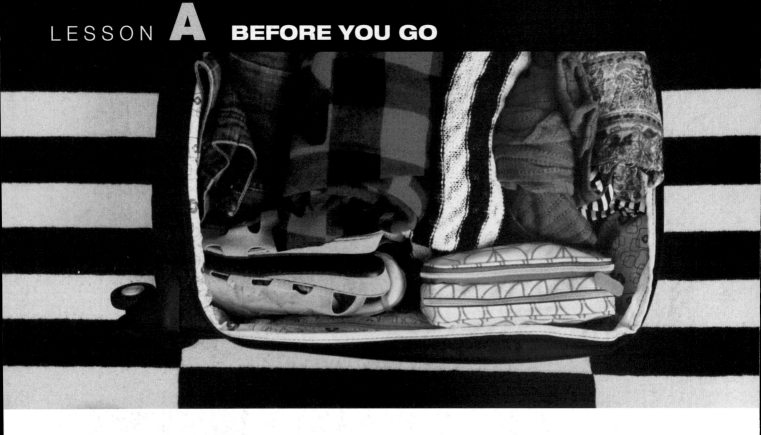

1 **VIDEO** Keeping Clean While Traveling

A Imagine you are on a trip and these situations happen to you. Read the sentences and look up any unfamiliar vocabulary. What would you do in each case? Tell a partner.

Your shoes get scuffed up.   Your toiletries spill in your bag.

You need to wash some clothes.

B Read the sentences and then watch the video. How does the woman deal with each situation? Choose the correct answers.

1. When your shoes get scuffed up, use _____ to clean them.

    a. a shoe-cleaning kit   b. vinegar

2. Keep your toiletries in _____.

    a. a ziplock plastic bag   b. a designer medicine bag

3. When you need to wash your clothes on a trip, use _____.

    a. laundry detergent packs   b. the hotel laundry service

4. When you get a stain on your clothing, use _____.

    a. laundry detergent packs   b. a stain remover pen

C Discuss the questions with a partner.

1. What do you think of the travel tips for keeping clean while traveling? Are they practical?

2. Can you add one more tip to the list?

2 VOCABULARY

A Andrew and Becky are going on a trip to visit some friends. What will they do before they leave home? Match 1–5 with a–e. Then match 6–10 with f–j.

1. **pack** e	a. the trash		6. **give** f	f. their house keys to a friend	
2. **empty** d	b. the weather		7. **lock** i	g. the plants	
3. **check** b	c. their bills		8. **turn off** h	h. the lights	
4. **give away** a	d. their suitcases		9. **confirm** j	i. the front door	
5. **pay** c	e. any fresh foods		10. **water** g	j. their flight plans	

B Look at the pictures. With a partner, talk about the tasks Andrew and Becky did before leaving on their trip. Take turns.

Andrew called to confirm their flight plans.

Becky called to...

I'm calling to confirm our flight to...

Hi, Jack, what's the weather like there?

Thank you. Here are the keys. Do you want this fruit?

I need to pay my...

C Discuss the questions with a partner.

1. Think about your travel experiences. Which tasks do you do before you leave home? When do you do them?

2. Have you ever forgotten to do one of the tasks in **A**? What happened?

I always pack my suitcase the night before I leave.

3 LISTENING

A 🔊 **Pronunciation: Reduced *have to* and *has to*.** Listen to the sentences. Notice the pronunciation of *have to* and *has to*. Then listen again and repeat. **CD 2 Track 41**

1. He has to lock the front door.
2. She still has to pack her suitcase.

3. We have to confirm our flight.
4. I have to find my passport!

B 🔊 **Listen for main ideas.** Listen to Paula's conversation about her trip. Then circle the correct answers. **CD 2 Track 42**

1. It's summer / winter now.
2. Paula is going to Hawaii / New York.
3. She's leaving tomorrow morning / afternoon.
4. She's traveling by herself / with other people.
5. She's calling Lewis to ask for help / advice.

C 🔊 **Listen for details.** Listen again. Who has to do each task? Write *P* for Paula, *L* for Lewis, or *X* if the task is not mentioned. **CD 2 Track 42**

1. pick up a package _____
2. pack _____
3. lock the door _____
4. check the weather _____

5. water the plants _____
6. empty the trash _____
7. confirm his or her flight plans _____
8. pay some bills _____

D 🔁 Check your answers in **C** with a partner. Take turns and pay attention to the pronunciation of *has to*.

> Paula has to...
>
> Lewis has to...

E 🔁 Do you ever ask your friends or neighbors for help? Why or why not? Discuss with a partner.

On a visit to Hawaii, you have to pack sunscreen and a swimsuit.

4 SPEAKING

A 🔊 Esther and Mina are preparing to leave on a trip. Listen to their conversation. What is the problem? **CD 2 Track 43**

ESTHER: We have to leave in 30 minutes. Have you finished packing?

MINA: Yes, I have...

ESTHER: You look worried. What's wrong?

MINA: I can't remember where I put my passport.

ESTHER: Oh, no!

MINA: It's here somewhere.

ESTHER: When did you last have it?

MINA: About ten minutes ago. Let me think... Oh, there it is. I put it on the dresser.

ESTHER: What a relief!

Many public places, such as airports and hotels, have Lost and Found offices. At the "Lost and Found," you can retrieve your lost items that were found by other people.

B 🔄 Practice the conversation with a partner.

C 🔄 Talk about a time when you lost something. What did you do? Tell a partner.

SPEAKING STRATEGY

D Study the Useful Expressions in the chart. Practice saying the sentences.

Useful Expressions	
Saying you've forgotten something	
I forgot + noun	I forgot my bus pass.
I forgot + infinitive	I forgot to empty the trash.
I don't remember + gerund	I don't remember turning off the lights.
I can't remember where + clause	I can't remember where I put my car keys.

E 🔄 You are going to perform a short conversation about forgetting something. Follow the steps below.

Step 1: Choose a location.

☐ the airport
☐ school
☐ the office

Step 2: Choose something you forgot to take or do.

☐ ticket   ☐ check the weather
☐ report   ☐ lock the door
☐ textbook   ☐ other: _____

Step 3: Write and practice a short conversation with your partner. Then perform it for the class.

OK, it's time to get on the plane.

Wait a minute! I think I forgot to lock the front door!

Oh, no! Can you call a friend for help?

5 GRAMMAR

A Turn to page 217. Complete the exercise. Then do **B–D** below.

Modal Verbs of Necessity		
	Present forms	**Past forms**
Affirmative	You **must** show your ID to get on the plane. I **have to** buy a backpack for my trip. We'**ve got to** get some cash.	I **had to** wait at the airport for an hour.
Negative	I don't **have to** check any luggage.	I didn't **have to** wait long.

Use *must, have to*, and *have got to* to say that something is necessary.

B 🔁 Look at the trip preparation to-do list. The tasks that are checked (✓) are finished. On a piece of paper, use the words in parentheses to write eight sentences with *has / have to* or *doesn't / don't have to*. Check your answers with a partner.

People hike on the Inca Trail in Peru.

To-Do List

buy a backpack (I)
✓ prepare a first-aid kit (she)
get a shot (he)
✓ renew passport (they)
confirm flight plans (we)
pack (she)
✓ check the weather (he)
✓ pay the bills (you)

> She doesn't have to prepare a first-aid kit. She's already done it.

C Complete each item with something that is true for you.

1. When I was younger, I had to...
2. Before you get on a plane, you must...
3. Before I leave home every day, I've got to...
4. I'm good at..., so I don't have to study it much.
5. The last time I took a trip, I didn't have to...
6. In order to pass this class, we have to...

D 🔁 Share your ideas in **C** with a partner.

> When I was younger, I had to be home early. I had a strict curfew.

> I had to be home by 8:00 every night.

> Really? What time was your curfew?

6 COMMUNICATION

A  Imagine you and your partner are going on a camping trip for three days. You will be in the forest, far away from any towns or cities. With your partner:

- Circle the items that are necessary for your trip.

- Check (✔) the items that you would like to bring but that are not necessary.

- Cross out the items that are not necessary.

a tent

sleeping bag   phone   flashlight   chewing gum   bottled water

canned food   backpack   Swiss Army knife   lighter   first-aid kit

thermos bottle   money   cooking pot   plastic plates and cups

B Join another pair. Together you must decide what to take on your trip. You can only take six items. Choose four items pictured above. Think of two more items. Consider these things:

- food   - shelter
- water   - safety

We've got to take the tent for shelter.

I like chewing gum, but we don't have to bring any.

C Tell the class the items your group has decided to take and explain your reasons.

CABULARY

A  Match a word on the left with one on the right to form compound nouns about air travel. Write each compound noun below the picture it describes. Then check your answers with a partner.

baggage	carry-on	flight	oxygen
boarding	check-in	overhead	~~tray~~

attendant	compartment	luggage	pass
claim	counter	mask	~~table~~

1. _____tray table_____

2. _____

3. _____

4. _____

5. _____

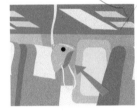

6. _____

7. _____

8. _____

B Use the compound words in **A** to complete the sentences below.

1. When you arrive at the airport for your flight, you go to the _____check-in counter_____ first.

2. You can bring _____ on the plane with you.

3. Before you get on the plane, you must show your _____.

4. When you enter the plane, you put your luggage in the _____.
   You may need to ask a _____ for help.

5. Before takeoff, you learn about safety. They show you how to use an _____.

6. During the flight, you are served drinks on your _____.

7. After the flight is over, you go to the _____ area to get your luggage.

C  With a partner, use the vocabulary items in **A** to role-play a dialog between a traveler and a person working at the airport. Then perform your dialog for another pair.

> Excuse me, this overhead
> compartment is full.

> May I check your bag for you?

2 LISTENING

A 🔊 **Listen for gist.** Jun and Ashley live in Japan. Read the sentence. Then listen and mark the correct answer. **CD 2 Track 44**

They are talking about a trip _____ took during the long weekend.

a. Ashley   b. Jun   c. they   d. their friends

B 🔊 **Listen to sequence events; Listen for details.** Look at the countries below. **CD 2 Track 44**

Then listen again and do the following:

1. Put the trip in order from the first (1) to the last place (4) visited. One place is extra.

2. Match each place with the activity or activities done there.

Word Bank

Travelers get *frequent flyer points* for flying with an airline often. Later, a person can use these points to get free flights.

During a trip, a *layover* is a short stop in another place before you go to your final destination.

A *long weekend* is a weekend plus an extra free day or two.

Places visited on the trip	Activity
_____ Singapore —————————	a. had breakfast
___1___ South Korea	b. went to the beach
_____ Vietnam	c. went shopping
_____ Thailand	d. visited a friend
_____ The Philippines	

C 🔊 **Infer information; Listen for details.** Listen again. Are the sentences below true or false? Circle the correct answer. Then write some notes to explain your answer. **CD 2 Track 44**

1. The luggage was a problem to carry.   True   False

_____

2. The trip was kind of expensive.   True   False

_____

D 🔄 Does Jun's trip sound like fun to you? Why or why not? Tell a partner.

Halong Bay, Vietnam

3 READING

GOING SOLO IS THE WAY TO GO!

A **Make predictions.** Read the title of the article and look quickly at the rest of the passage. Answer the question below. Then read the article. Was your prediction correct?

What do you think the author is writing about? Check (✓) your answer.

☐ 1. the advantages of traveling alone

☐ 2. memories of traveling alone

☐ 3. the cost of traveling alone

B 🗩 **Guess meaning from context.** Reread the second paragraph. What do you think *striking out on their own* means? Tell a partner.

C **Read for details.** Read the article again. What does it mention about solo travel? Check (✓) your answers.

☐ 1. the cost of solo travel

☐ 2. the dangers of traveling alone

☐ 3. study vacations

☐ 4. learning a sport

☐ 5. packing for a trip alone

☐ 6. options for solo travelers

☐ 7. carry-on luggage

☐ 8. making friends

D **Scan for details.** Look at the items you checked in **C**. For each item, give examples from the reading.

1. _____

2. _____

3. _____

4. _____

E 🗩 Discuss the questions with a partner.

1. Would you like to take a vacation by yourself? Why or why not?

2. What other tips can you think of for a solo traveler?

How do you usually travel? Do you go with a close friend or a group of friends? Do you join a tour group? Do you travel with your family?

Have you ever thought about "going solo"? In recent years, more and more people have started striking out on their own. You may think that traveling alone would be scary or boring. Well, according to people who do it, that's not exactly true. Solo travelers often have positive experiences: They make new friends, get to know themselves better, and can make their own schedules for flights, hotels, and meals.

There are many different things you can do on a vacation alone. Some solo travelers use the time to learn or practice a sport such as golf, mountain climbing, or scuba diving. Others go and stay on a ranch and learn how to ride a horse. You can pretend to be a cowboy or a cowgirl for a day!

You may not believe this, but some travelers like to study on their vacation. They even go to "vacation college" at a university or join a research team as a volunteer worker. It's hard but satisfying work. You can "play scientist" for a week or two while you help someone with his or her project.

For solo travelers of different ages and genders, there are many travel options. There are tours for women only and for people over the age of 60 where the tour company does things like help travelers with all of their baggage. And, of course, there are trips for singles who are looking for romance. One company offers trips that focus on fine dining—there is time for sightseeing during the day and for sharing a delicious meal with new friends at night.

So for your next vacation, if you haven't considered going solo, think about it!

Bon voyage!

Many people hike Pha Tang Mountain in Thailand to see beautiful views of Thailand, Laos, and the Mekong River.

4 GRAMMAR

A Turn to page 217. Complete the exercises. Then do **B** and **C** below.

Present Perfect (Indefinite Time) vs. Simple Past		
Statements	I**'ve been** to Korea.	He**'s booked** his flight.

Questions and answers	**Have** you (<u>ever</u>) **been** to Brazil?
	   Yes, I have. I **was** there last year.*
	   No, I haven't.
	   No, I've <u>never</u> been there.
		Have you **packed** <u>yet</u>?
		   Yes, I've <u>already</u> packed.
		   Yes, I've packed <u>already</u>.
		   No, I haven't packed <u>yet</u>. / No, not yet.

Remember: When you answer a present perfect question with a specific time expression, use the <u>simple past</u>.

B Follow the steps below.

1. Complete expressions 1–8 below with the correct past participle. Then use the present perfect to ask your classmates if they have done each activity.

2. When someone answers *Yes* to a question, ask a follow-up question. Then write the person's name and the extra piece of information. Try to be the first person to complete 1–8.

> Jin Sung, have you ever visited a big city?

> Yes, I have.

> Which city?

> Seoul.

Find someone who has…

		Name	Information
1. (visit) _visited_ a big city		_____	_____
2. (be) _____ on a train		_____	_____
3. (talk) _____ to a flight attendant		_____	_____
4. (forget) _____ something on a trip		_____	_____
5. (go) _____ to the beach		_____	_____
6. (lose) _____ their luggage		_____	_____
7. (get) _____ sick while traveling		_____	_____
8. (miss) _____ a flight, train, or bus		_____	_____

C Listen to your instructor read each item in **B**. If you've ever done the activity, raise your hand.

5 WRITING

A Read about homesharing websites. Have you, or someone you know, ever used one of these sites to travel? Do you think it's a good idea? Tell a partner.

Hotels can be expensive. That's why more travelers are using homesharing websites to find a cheaper place to stay. Using these sites, home owners (hosts) can rent rooms or entire homes to travelers from around the world. These rentals are usually affordable.

How it works: Travelers go on a site, choose a place to stay, and then send the host a message introducing themselves.

B 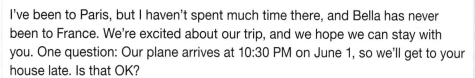 Chloe (a host) lives in Paris. She is renting a room in her home. Amelia (a traveler) wants to rent the room. Read Amelia's message to Chloe. Answer the questions with a partner.

1. Who is Amelia traveling with? When are they going?

2. What are Amelia and Bella like?

3. Have they ever been to Paris?

4. What is Amelia's question?

Hi Chloe,

My name is Amelia, and I'm from Argentina. My friend Bella and I plan to visit Paris June 1–5 on vacation. We saw your apartment, and it looks perfect because it is right in the city center. Here's a little about us: We're both 21, we're students, and we love to travel!

I've been to Paris, but I haven't spent much time there, and Bella has never been to France. We're excited about our trip, and we hope we can stay with you. One question: Our plane arrives at 10:30 PM on June 1, so we'll get to your house late. Is that OK?

Looking forward to hearing from you!

Amelia

C Go to a homesharing site on the Internet. Choose a place to visit. Then use the example and questions 1–3 in **B** to write a short message on a piece of paper introducing yourself to the host. If necessary, ask questions, too.

D Exchange papers with a partner.

1. Where is your partner going? Answer questions 1–3 in **B** about your partner.

2. Circle any mistakes in your partner's message. Then return the paper to your partner. Make changes to your own message.

6 COMMUNICATION

Amelia? Hi, I'm Chloe.

A With a partner, choose one of your travel plans from Writing and role-play a meeting between the traveler and the host.

TRAVELER: You arrive late to the host's home. Explain why. Talk about your plans for your trip.

HOST: Welcome your guest. Ask him or her three *Have you (ever)* questions in the role play.

Nice to meet you, Chloe. Sorry I'm late. I had to wait a long time in baggage claim.

No problem. Have you eaten dinner yet?

B Perform your role play for another pair.

No, I haven't, and I'm hungry!

C Switch partners and repeat **A** and **B**.

1 STORYBOARD

A Pia is calling Bob, her boss, at work. Complete the conversations. For some blanks, more than one answer is possible.

B In groups of three, practice the conversations. Then change roles and practice again.

C Think of an interesting place to make a telephone call from. Then make your own conversation like the one above. Practice with your group.

2 SEE IT AND SAY IT

A Look at the picture of Leo's house. He went on a trip, but he forgot to do many things before he left. On a piece of paper, make a list of what he forgot to do.

B  Work with a partner. Pretend that you are Leo and call a friend. Choose three things you forgot to do and ask for help. Then switch roles.

> I don't remember turning off the light in the living room. Can you do it for me?

> Sure. No problem.

3 A TV AD

A 🔄 Read the ad. Circle the correct answer(s) in the sentences. Then unscramble the adjectives. Check your answers with a partner.

This Week's Best Buy!

50 in / 127 cm

★ **Are you planning** buying / to buy **a new TV?**

★ **Do you hate** watching / to watch **movies on a small screen?**

★ **When you watch sports, do you want** feeling / to feel **like you're actually at the game?**

★ **Would you like** saving / to save **energy when you watch TV?**

Try our new flat screen HDTV!

And you'll appreciate watching / to watch **TV in a whole new way!**

★ (beerraakml) _____ picture quality!

★ (fabfadrole) _____ -Now only $900!

★ (dealurb) _____ -Guaranteed to last 20 years!

B 🔄 With a partner, compare your TV to the one in the ad using *(not) as... as.*

> My TV isn't as expensive as the TV in the ad.

4 OLD FAVORITES

A Complete the chart with your favorites.

	When you were younger	Now
Snack food		
Music group or singer		
Piece of clothing you own(ed)		
Hobby		
Weekend activities		

B 🔄 With a partner, ask and answer questions about your present and past favorites. Use *used to* for the past favorites. Have you changed a lot?

> What snack food did you use to eat?

> I used to eat a lot of sweets, but these days, I eat healthier snacks.

5 FIRST TRIP

A Emma Goldstein is 90 years old. She took her first trip on an airplane last month. Read what she said. Then correct the mistake(s) in each sentence. They can be mistakes in grammar or vocabulary. Some sentences can be fixed more than one way.

1. I used to ~~was~~ ^{be} afraid of flying.

2. Last month, I made a call from my daughter.

3. She said, "You must to pack your bags. We're taking a trip."

4. I didn't want to going at first because I disliked to fly.

5. I took two pieces of boarding passes on the plane.

6. The flight attendant was nice. She helped me put everything in the oxygen mask.

7. Airplane travel is not as scarier as I thought.

8. I can now proudly say, "I have flying on an airplane!"

B 🔁 Ask your partner about a trip he or she has taken.

6 LISTENING

A 🔊 Read the phone messages below. Then listen and circle the correct answer for each question. **CD 2 Track 46**

1. Which message did Sheila leave for Tom?

WHILE YOU WERE OUT	WHILE YOU WERE OUT	WHILE YOU WERE OUT
Sheila called. She wants to meet soon. She will call again at 5:00.	Sheila called. She can't meet tomorrow. Please call her.	Sheila called. She can't meet today. She wants to meet tomorrow at 2:00.

2. Which message did Ted leave for Penny's brother?

WHILE YOU WERE OUT	WHILE YOU WERE OUT	WHILE YOU WERE OUT
Ted called. His computer crashed and won't start. He wants you to fix it. Can you call him? His number is 555-9083.	Ted called. He has a question about his new laptop. Please call him back.	Ted called. He wants you to help him buy a new computer. He'll call you later.

UNIT **1** MY LIFE

LESSON A

Vocabulary

friend
We're good / close / best / old friends.

acquaintance
I don't know her (very) well. / She's just an acquaintance.

girlfriend / boyfriend
We're dating. / We're seeing each other. / We're going out.

coworker / colleague
We work together. / We're in the same department / office.

neighbor
We're next-door neighbors.

classmate
We're in the same class. / We go to the same school.

Speaking Strategy

Introducing a person to someone else
Mr. Otani, I'd like to introduce you to Andres.
Mr. Otani, I'd like you to meet Andres.
Junko, this is Ricardo.
Junko, meet Ricardo.
Junko, Ricardo.

Responding to introductions
It's (very) nice to meet you.
(It's) nice / good to meet you, too.
Nice / Good to meet you. You, too.

LESSON B

Vocabulary

get a (good) **grade**
have (baseball, soccer) **practice**
meet
pass ↔ **fail**
prepare (for something)
take (music, swimming, tennis) **lessons**
take a (class, test) / **an exam**
tutor
win, won, winner ↔ lose, lost, loser

failure (*n.*), fail (*v.*) ↔ success (*n.*)
succeed (*v.*), successful (*adj.*)
give up (quit) ↔ keep trying

UNIT **2** LET'S EAT!

LESSON A

Vocabulary

baked
delicious / tasty / yummy ↔ **awful / terrible**
farmers' market
fried
frozen
grilled
juicy
oily
salty
spicy ↔ **mild**
sweet ↔ **sour / bitter**

Speaking Strategy

Making suggestions
Let's have Thai food for dinner.
Why don't we have Thai food for dinner?
How about having Thai food for dinner?

Responding to suggestions
Good / Great idea!
(That) sounds good (to me).
(That's) fine with me.
I don't really want to.
I don't really feel like it.

LESSON B

Vocabulary

benefit
cut back on ↔ **increase** (something)
a (healthy) **diet**
a (traditional) dish
eliminate
fast food
a (bad / unhealthy) **habit**
lifestyle
member
movement
plenty (of something)
protect (you from something)

UNIT 3 MYSTERIES

LESSON A

Vocabulary

lucky ↔ unlucky
good luck ↔ bad luck
(do something) on purpose ↔
    (happen) by chance
facts ↔ intuition

take a chance (= risk)
by chance (= luck)
increase your chances
    (= opportunities)

Speaking Strategy

Talking about possibility
Saying something is likely
I bet (that) Marco plays the
    drums.
Marco probably plays the drums.
Maybe / Perhaps Marco plays the
    drums.

Saying something is not likely
I doubt (that) Marco plays the
    drums.

LESSON B

Vocabulary

affect
behavior
explanation
figure (something) **out**
figure out (why something
    happens)
Experts / Scientists say / think /
    believe (that)...
In fact...
investigate
mysterious
make sense
(have / need / show / there's no)
    proof
solve (a problem / a mystery)
(have a) **theory**

UNIT 4 TRENDS

LESSON A

Vocabulary

trend

increase / rise ↔ decrease /
    fall / drop
over / more than ↔ under / less
    than

exactly / precisely
approximately / about / around
nearly / almost

a couple
one half
two thirds
percent
twice as high as...
three times as many as...
typical

Speaking Strategy

Disagreeing
I know what you're saying, but...
I see what you mean, but...
Yes, (that may be true), but...
I'm not so sure about that.

Disagreeing more strongly
I'm afraid I disagree.
Sorry, but I disagree.
That's (just) not true.
I totally / completely disagree.

LESSON B

Vocabulary

a **look** / style
(to be) in (style)

Types of clothing
baggy / oversized ↔ fitted
    (shirt, pants, jeans)
pointy (shoes)
ripped (jeans)
skinny

Describing personal style
casual / comfortable ↔
    formal / conservative
colorful
dramatic / flashy ↔ plain /
    simple
retro / vintage
stylish / elegant
sporty
unique / unusual ↔ common /
    ordinary

UNIT 5 OUT AND ABOUT

LESSON A

Vocabulary

do the dishes
do laundry
drop off (your sister)
go grocery shopping
make a reservation (at a restaurant)
make a (doctor's) **appointment**
make dinner
pick up (your sister)
sweep (the floor)
vacuum (the rugs)

Speaking Strategy

Making appointments
Explaining why you're calling
I'm calling to… / I'd like to…
   make an appointment with a counselor / Dr. Smith / the dentist.
   make a dentist / doctor's / hair appointment.
   reschedule my appointment / our meeting.

Scheduling the time
Can you come in / Could we meet / How's tomorrow at 2:00?
   That's perfect. / That works for me.
   No, that (time / day) doesn't work for me.

LESSON B

Vocabulary

get around (on foot)
get to (a place)
lane
pedestrian
sidewalk
traffic
walkable

by / on + transportation		verbs
by	bike / scooter	ride your bike / scooter
	bus / subway	take the bus / subway
	car	drive
	taxi	take a taxi
	train	take / catch the train
on	foot	walk

UNIT 6 GOALS

LESSON A

Vocabulary

apply → **application**
compete → **competition**
consider → **consideration**
decide → **decision**
observe → **observation**
recommend → **recommendation**

Speaking Strategy

Responding to bad news
(I'm) sorry to hear that.
That's too bad.
How disappointing.
You must be disappointed.

Offering to help
If you want to talk, (just) call me.
If there's anything I can do, (just) let me know.

LESSON B

Vocabulary

be (your) own boss
a catch
create a résumé
do an internship
go back to school
mentor
opportunity
take a risk / take risks
take (time) off
(a school) term

Talking about indefinite future time
at some point
in a few (days, weeks)
soon
in the near future
someday / eventually

UNIT 7 CELEBRATIONS

LESSON A

Vocabulary

attend / go to
have / host / throw } a party
organize / plan
celebrate → celebration
decorate → decoration
fan
get together
guest
have a good time
inspiration
invite → invitation
live
occasion

Speaking Strategy

Inviting someone to do something
Do you want / Would you like /
How'd you like to go with me?

Accepting an invitation
Sure, I'd love to.
That sounds great.

Refusing an invitation
I'm sorry, but I can't. I have
  plans.
Unfortunately, I can't. I have to
  work.
I'd love to, but I'm busy (then /
  that day).

LESSON B

Vocabulary

compete → competitor →
  competition
gather
participate → participant →
  participation
perform → performer →
  performance
(win a) prize
race
take place
tradition

UNIT 8 STORYTELLING

LESSON A

Vocabulary

a **character** in a story
based on
the beginning / end of a story
easy ↔ hard to follow
fantasy
heartbreaking
heartwarming
(happy) ending
made-up (land)
make up a story
series
The story is about... / It tells
  the story of...
tell a story
true
(un)predictable
(un)realistic
uplifting
violent

Speaking Strategy

Keeping a story going
One day,...
So, (then),...
Later,...
After that,...
As it turns out,...
It turns out that,...

LESSON B

Vocabulary

arrogant
clever
discover (+ *that* + sentence)
eloquent
incredible
overcome (a problem)
patient
quick ↔ slow
struggle (to do something)
survive

UNIT 9 WORK

LESSON A

Vocabulary

adventurous
cautious
courageous
efficient
flexible
independently
knowledgeable
personable
punctual
responsible

Speaking Strategy

Interviewing for a job

Starting the Interview
Thanks for coming in today.
　　It's great to be here. / My
　　pleasure.

Discussing abilities and experience
Tell me a little bit about yourself.
　　I'm a first-year university
　　student.
　　I'm majoring in journalism.

Can you (work independently)?
　　Yes, I can. For example,…

Are you (punctual)?
　　Yes, I am. For example,…

Do you have any experience
　　(writing a blog)?
　　Yes, I write one for my school
　　newspaper now.

Ending the interview
Do you have any questions?
　　Yes, I do. / No, I don't think so.

When can you start?
　　Right away. / On Monday. /
　　Next week.

I'll be in touch.
　　I look forward to hearing
　　from you.

LESSON B

Vocabulary

demanding
dull ↔ glamorous
exhausting
hazardous
job / career / profession
passion
passionate (about something)
rewarding ↔ unsatisfying
well-paid ↔ dead-end

UNIT 10 TELEPHONING

LESSON A

Vocabulary

Phrases with *phone*

answer the phone ↔ hang up
  the phone
be on the phone / talk on the
  phone
borrow / use someone's phone
mute / silence your phone
turn on your phone ↔ turn off
  your phone

Phrases with *call*

call someone / make a call
call someone back / return
  a call
get a call from someone
screen your calls

Phrases with *message*

check your (text / phone)
  messages
get a (text / phone) message ↔
  leave a message / send a
  message
take a message

Speaking Strategy

Using the telephone

Asking for someone and
  responding
Hi, Lisa? / Hi. Is Lisa there?
Hello. May / Could / Can I speak
  to Lisa, please? [formal]
This is Lisa. / Speaking.

Asking for identification of caller
Who's calling?
May I ask who's calling? [formal]

Asking someone to wait
Hang on. / Can you hang on (for a
  moment / second)?
Would / Could you hold (for a
  moment / second)? [formal]

Taking a message
Can I take a message?
May I take a message? [formal]
Would you like to leave a
  message? [formal]

LESSON B

Vocabulary

add / post ↔ **delete**
(be) addicted (to something)
at the last minute
ban ↔ **allow**
bullying
polite ↔ **rude**
raise your voice ↔ **lower your**
  voice
respond ↔ **ignore**
thoughtless ↔ **thoughtful**
turn down (the music) ↔ **turn**
  up (the music)
turn down (a request) ↔ **accept**
  (a request)

Come on.
I mean…
Look…

UNIT 11 TECHNOLOGY

LESSON A

Vocabulary

affordable
dependable
durable
fad
fashionable
features
flash in the pan
manageable
portable
practical
product
reliable
remarkable

Speaking Strategy

Offering a counterargument
Stating what other people think
A lot of people say (that)…
Some people think (that) (she's really shy).

Explaining what you think
(But,) actually,…
(But,) in fact, / in reality,…
(But,) the truth / fact / reality is (she's very outgoing).

LESSON B

Vocabulary

consume
have a(n) (positive / negative) **effect**
located
prevent
recycle
reduce
rescue
restore
transform

UNIT 12 TRAVEL

LESSON A

Vocabulary

check the (weather)
confirm (my flight plans)
empty (the trash)
give away (any fresh foods)
give (my house keys to a friend)
lock (the front door)
pack (your suitcase)
pay (some bills)
turn off (the lights)
water (the plants)

Speaking Strategy

Saying you've forgotten something
I forgot + noun:
I forgot my bus pass.
I forgot + infinitive:
I forgot to empty the trash.

I don't remember + gerund:
I don't remember turning off the lights.

I can't remember where + clause:
I can't remember where I put my car keys.

LESSON B

Vocabulary

baggage claim
boarding pass
carry-on luggage
check-in counter
flight attendant
frequent flyer miles
layover
long weekend
overhead compartment
oxygen mask
tray table

UNIT **1** MY LIFE

LESSON A

The Simple Present Tense vs. the Present Continuous Tense	
Simple present	**Present continuous**
Use the simple present to talk about habits, schedules, and facts.	Use the present continuous to talk about actions that are happening right now*.
I always **take** a shower in the morning. The express train **arrives** at 9:03 AM. They **don't speak** Italian. They **speak** French.	She**'s taking** a shower. Can she call you back? Hurry up! The train **is leaving**! Look at me! I**'m speaking** to you!
Sometimes the simple present and the present continuous have similar meanings, but use of the present continuous can show a situation is more temporary.	
I **live** in Taipei. A: Every summer, my family goes to the beach. B: Nice! **Do** you **stay** in a hotel?	At the moment, I**'m living** in Taipei. A: Let's have lunch at my hotel. B: Sounds good. Where **are** you **staying**?
	*Also use the present continuous to talk about actions happening in the extended present (nowadays). Notice the <u>time expressions</u>.
	How many classes **are** you **taking** <u>this term</u>? She **is living** in Singapore <u>these days</u>.

A Veronique Lesarg is a doctor. Use the simple present or present continuous to complete her profile.

My name (1. be) _____ Veronique Lesarg. I (2. live) _____ in Montreal.

I (3. be) _____ a pediatrician, a doctor for children. I usually (4. work) _____

in a hospital, but these days, I (5. volunteer) _____ for an organization called

Doctors Without Borders. They (6. send) _____ staff to other countries. This year,

I (7. work) _____ in Africa. At the moment, I (8. write) _____ to you from

a small village. There's no hospital here, so right now we (9. build) _____ one.

B Write two simple present and two present continuous questions about Veronique Lesarg.

1. _____   3. _____

2. _____   4. _____

LESSON B

Review of the Simple Past Tense				
Subject	**Verb**		**Time expressions**	
I You	**missed** *didn't miss*	a tennis lesson	yesterday. two days / weeks ago. last week / month.	The past tense ending of regular verbs is *-ed*. For irregular verbs, see the list below.
He / She We They	**had** *didn't have*			

	Yes / No questions	**Answers**
With *be*	Were you in class today?	Yes, I was. / No, I wasn't.
With other verbs	Did you pass the test?	Yes, I did. / No, I didn't.
	Wh- questions	**Answers**
With *be*	Where were you last night?	(I was) at my friend's house.
With other verbs	When did you meet your girlfriend?	(We met) last year.

Regular Past Tense Verbs				Irregular Past Tense Verbs			
Base form	**Past tense**	**Base form**	**Past tense**	**Base form**	**Past tense**	**Base form**	**Past tense**
change	changed	pass	passed	be	was / were	know	knew
die	died	play	played	come	came	make	made
enter	entered	prepare	prepared	do	did	meet	met
finish	finished	practice	practiced	eat	ate	read	read
graduate	graduated	study	studied	give	gave	run	ran
help	helped	talk	talked	get	got	take	took
live	lived	travel	traveled	go	went	think	thought
marry	married	use	used	have	had	win	won
move	moved	work	worked	keep	kept	write	wrote

A Read about Diego's experience. Complete the sentences with the correct simple past tense forms of the verbs in parentheses.

In high school, I (1. study) _____ a lot and got good grades. But the first time I (2. take) _____ the university entrance exam, I (3. fail) _____. That (4. be) _____ hard. To prepare for the next exam, I (5. go) _____ to a test prep center. Two good things (6. happen) _____ there: I (7. meet) _____ my girlfriend in the class. And the next time I (8. take) _____ the entrance exam, I (9. pass) _____ it!

B Write six past tense questions about Diego. Then answer them on a separate piece of paper.

1. *Was Diego a good student in high school?* _____
2. _____
3. _____
4. _____
5 _____
6. _____

C Write sentences about things you did or didn't do yesterday. Use the verb phrases provided.

1. go to school   _I didn't go to school yesterday. I was sick._

2. study for a test   _____

3. do homework   _____

4. practice English   _____

Did you go to school yesterday?

No, I didn't.

Why not? What did you do?

D 🔁 Ask a partner *Yes / No* questions to learn his or her answers in **C**. Then ask a follow-up *Wh-* question.

I stayed home. I was sick.

UNIT **2** LET'S EAT!

LESSON A

The Comparative Form of Adjectives	
This restaurant is **bigger than** that one.	Use the comparative form of an adjective to compare two things.
Your cooking is **better than** my mom's. My cold is **worse** today **than** it was yesterday.	The comparative of *good* is *better*. The comparative of *bad* is *worse*.
I'm tall, but Milo is **taller**.	Sometimes, you can use the comparative form without *than*.

One syllable	sweet → sweet**er**	Add *-er* to many one-syllable adjectives.
	large → large**r**	Add *-r* if the adjective ends in *-e*.
	big → big**ger**	Double the final consonant and add *-er* if the adjective ends in a vowel + consonant.
Two syllables	simple → simple**r** quiet → quiet**er**	Add *-r* or *-er* to two-syllable adjectives that end in an unstressed syllable.
	spicy → spic**ier**	Change the final *-y* to *-ier* if the adjective ends in *-y*.
	crowded → **more** crowded famous → **more** famous	Add *more* to other adjectives, especially those ending in *-ing*, *-ed*, *-ous*, or *-ful*.
Three syllables	relaxing → **more** relaxing delicious → **more** delicious	Add *more* to all adjectives with three or more syllables.

A Write the comparative form of the adjectives.

1. mild   _____   6. big   _____

2. tasty   _____   7. good   _____

3. popular   _____   8. comfortable   _____

4. hungry   _____   9. nice   _____

5. bad   _____   10. expensive   _____

B Read the facts. Then make a sentence using the comparative followed by *than*.

> Use *than* after the comparative when the two things being compared are mentioned in the same sentence: *The popcorn is saltier than the pretzels.*

A can of regular cola has 44 grams of sugar.

A can of diet cola has 0 grams of sugar.

1. (sweet) _____

Some people like baked chicken.

Everyone loves grilled chicken.

2. (popular) _____

Korean dishes are very spicy.

English dishes are not so spicy.

3. (spicy) _____

The streets in the village are empty.

There are a lot of cars on the streets in the city.

4. (busy) _____

It costs $30 to eat at the French restaurant.

It costs $10 to eat at the coffee shop.

5. (expensive) _____

LESSON B

The Superlative Form of Adjectives	
It's **the oldest** restaurant in Paris. (= The other restaurants are not as old.)	Use the superlative form of an adjective to compare something to an entire group.
It's **one of the oldest** restaurants in Paris. (= It's one of many old restaurants in Paris.)	Use *one of…* to show that something or someone is part of a group.
Mario's has **the best** pizza in the city. It was **the worst** movie of the year.	The superlative of *good* is *the best*. The superlative of *bad* is *the worst*.

One syllable	sweet → **the** sweet**est** large → **the** larg**est**	Add *the* and *-est* or *-st* to many one-syllable adjectives.
Two syllables	quiet → **the** quiet**est** simple → **the** simpl**est**	Add *the* and *-est* or *-st* to two-syllable adjectives that end in an unstressed syllable.
	spicy → **the** spic**iest**	Add *the* and change the final *-y* to *-iest* if the adjective ends in *-y*.
	crowded → **the most** crowded famous → **the most** famous	Add *the most* to other adjectives, especially those ending in *-ing*, *-ed*, *-ous*, or *-ful*.
Three syllables	relaxing → **the most** relaxing delicious → **the most** delicious	Add *the most* to all adjectives with three or more syllables.

A Write the superlative form of the adjectives.

1. cheap _____
2. healthy _____
3. nervous _____
4. friendly _____
5. bad _____

6. unusual _____
7. good _____
8. helpful _____
9. tasty _____
10. expensive _____

B Complete the questions with the superlative form of the adjectives in parentheses.

1. Who is _____ (healthy) person in your family?
2. What is _____ (expensive) restaurant in your city?
3. What is _____ (good) food to eat when you're sick?
4. Who is _____ (popular) celebrity chef today?
5. What is _____ (bad) tasting food or drink?
6. What is _____ (hard) food or drink to eliminate from your diet?

C Take turns asking and answering the questions in **B** with a partner.

UNIT 3 MYSTERIES

LESSON A

Stative Verbs

Stative verbs describe states and feelings (not actions).

agree	belong	hate	like	mind	prefer
appear	dislike	hear	love	need	seem
believe	doubt	know	mean	own	want

Usually, they are not used in the present continuous tense.

He **seems** like a nice guy.	~~He is seeming like a nice guy.~~

Some stative verbs, however, can be used in the continuous. When used this way, their meaning changes.

Do you **think** he's lucky? (*think* = believe)	I'm **thinking** about it. (*think* = consider)
He **looks** happy. (*look* = appear)	Who **is looking** in the window? (*look* = direct eyes toward)
She **has** a lucky object. (*has* = own; possess)	They**'re having** coffee. (*have* = drink)
	Are you **having** fun? (*have* = experience)
I can't **see** without my glasses. (*see* = view with eyes)	I'm **seeing** her tomorrow. (*see* = meet)
I **see** what you mean. (*see* = understand)	

When you ask about how someone feels, you can use either form with no change in meaning.

How do you **feel**?	How **are** you **feeling**?

A Circle the correct answer to complete each sentence. (In one case, both answers are possible.)

1. I bet that lucky people have / are having more friends.

2. Do you think / Are you thinking some people are just luckier in life?

3. Lucky charms seem / are seeming to really work.

4. I think / I'm thinking about this statement: It's better to be lucky than smart.

5. I doubt / I'm doubting it's a fact.

6. I hear / I'm hearing that Professor Wiseman is a well-known psychologist.

7. It looks / is looking like Amy called me at 2:00.

8. A: Do you belong / Are you belonging to the International Student Club?

    B: Yes. Do you know / Are you knowing that we have / we're having a party next week?

9. A: How do you feel? / How are you feeling?

    B: I have / I'm having a cold.

10. I see / I'm seeing my best friend tomorrow. We have / We're having lunch together.

LESSON B

Modals of Present Possibility		
Subject	**Modal**	**Main verb**	
The Loch Ness Monster	**may / might / could**	be	real. Maybe it's a large animal.
	can't		real. There are no sea monsters.

You can use *may*, *might*, and *could* to say something is possible in the present tense.
Use *can't* to say something is impossible.
You can use *may* or *might* with *not*: **He might / may not** speak French.
Do not use *could* with *not* for present possibility.

Questions and Short Answers		
With *be*	Is the Loch Ness Monster real?	It **may / might / could** be.
With other verbs	Does the full moon affect us?	It **may / might / could**.

A Complete the dialogs with a modal and a verb if needed.

1. A: How old is Karen?

    B: I don't know. She _____ 35.

    C: She _____ be 35. She graduated from college in 1980.

2. A: Do ghosts exist?

    B: They _____. No one knows for sure.

3. A: Where's Lauren?

    B: I'm not sure. She _____ with Lin. They always hang out together after school.

    A: She _____ be with Lin. Lin is on vacation.

4. A: Are the Nazca Lines a type of calendar?

    B: They _____. It's one possible explanation.

B Read each situation. Write two possible explanations for each one on a piece of paper.

1. Your friend isn't answering her phone.
2. You received a mysterious package in the mail.
3. The teacher isn't here today.
4. A new student in class is very quiet.

C Work with a partner. Follow the steps below.

1. **Student A:** Tell your partner one situation in **B**.
2. **Student B:** Give a possible reason, using one of your sentences in **B**.
3. **Student A:** Answer with a negative modal.
4. **Student B:** Give your second idea.
5. Change roles and repeat steps 1–4. Do this until you talk about all the situations in **B**.

> My friend isn't answering her phone.

> Her phone might be off.

> It can't be. She called me two minutes ago.

> Oh, then she may be...

UNIT **4** TRENDS

LESSON A

Quantity Expressions with Specific Nouns				
Quantity word	*of*	**Determiner***	**Plural count noun**	
All **Most** **A lot** **Half** **Some** **None**	of	my	friends	live at home.
		Pronoun		
		them		

Use these quantity expressions to talk about amounts with **specific** nouns.

They can also be used with noncount nouns: *Half of my <u>homework</u> is finished.*

The word *of* is optional after *all* when it is followed by a determiner and a noun: *All (of) my friends live at home.*

*A determiner is a small word like *the*, *that*, or *my*.

Quantity Expressions with General Nouns		
Quantity word	**Plural count noun**	
All **Most** **A lot of** **Some**	students	study hard.

100% ↑ all / most / a lot / half / some
0% none

Use *all*, *most*, *a lot of*, and *some* followed by a noun to make **general** statements about people or things everywhere.

These expressions can also be used with noncount nouns: *Most water is clean.*

A Complete the sentences with the correct word(s). Some items may have more than one correct answer.

1. Some / Some of people want to be happy in life.
2. Most / Most of my friends speak English, but none / none of them speak it at home.
3. Some / Some of students live with their families because it's cheaper.
4. Half / Half of our neighbors have children. A couple / couple of them have pets, too.
5. All / All of parents want their children to do well in school.
6. All / All of the instructors at my school are really strict.

B Do you agree with the sentences in **A**? Rewrite them by changing the quantity words as necessary.

LESSON B

Giving Advice with *could*, *should*, *ought to*, and *had better*	
You **could** wear a dress to the party. You **could** wear the blue dress or the black one.	Use *could* to make a suggestion or give advice. It is often used to offer two or more choices.
You **should / ought to** wear a formal suit to the job interview. You **shouldn't** wear jeans. They're too casual.	Use *should* or *ought to* to give advice. Both are stronger than *could*. Use *shouldn't* in the negative.
You**'d better** wear a coat. It's going to rain. We**'d better not** drive to the concert. It will be hard to park.	Use *had better (not)* to give strong advice. It sounds like a warning or order. Use the contracted form (*you'd better*) in speaking.

Use *could*, *should*, *ought to*, or *had better* to give advice about something in the present or the near future.
These are all followed by the base form of a verb: *You could / should / ought to / had better wear a suit.*

A Complete the conversations with the expressions in the boxes. Use each expression only once.

shouldn't   could   ought to

A: I don't know what to wear to the party tonight.

B: You (1.) _____ wear your new skinny jeans or black pants.

A: It's a formal dinner party.

B: Oh, then you (2.) _____ wear jeans. They're too casual. You definitely
(3.) _____ wear the black pants.

could   had better not   had better

A: I still don't understand this grammar.

B: You (4.) _____ get some help. The test is on Thursday.

A: Maybe I (5.) _____ take the test on Friday. That would give me extra time.

B: Well, talk to the teacher, but you (6.) _____ delay. There's not much time!

UNIT 5 OUT AND ABOUT

LESSON A

Requests with Modal Verbs and *mind*				
Making requests				**Responding to requests**
Informal	**Can** / **Will** you **Could** / **Would** you	help	me, please?	OK. / Sure, no problem. / I'd be glad to. / Certainly. / Of course. Sorry, but…
Formal	**Would you mind**	helping		No, not at all. / No, I'd be glad to. Sorry, but…

Use *Can you*, *Will you*, *Could you*, or *Would you* + verb to make requests.

To make a formal request, use *Would you mind* + verb + *-ing*. Note: To agree to a *Would you mind…* request, answer with *No. (No, I don't mind.)*

To make a request more polite, add *please*.

A You need help preparing for a surprise birthday party. Read each sentence. Then use the words in parentheses to write a request.

1. There are a lot of dirty dishes in the sink. (could / do)
   Could you do the dishes, please?

2. You need something at the grocery store. (would / mind / go)
   _____

3. The rugs are dirty. (can / vacuum)
   _____

4. You don't have enough snacks. (would / make)
   _____

5. You need some flowers. (will / buy)
   _____

6. Someone needs to watch the soup on the stove. (would / mind / watch)
   _____

7. The birthday cake is still at the pastry shop. (could / pick up)
   _____

8. You need to blow up the birthday balloons. (would / mind / blow up)
   _____

B On a separate piece of paper, write a different response to each request.

LESSON B

Modifiers *really / very* and *pretty*			
	Adverb	**Adjective**	
It's	**really / very** **pretty**	far	from here.
		Adverb	**Adjective + noun**	
It's	a	**really / very** **pretty**	long walk	from here.
	Adverb	**Adverb**	
You speak English	**really / very** **pretty**	well.	

Really and *very* make adjectives and adverbs stronger. Compare:

My house is far from here. It's 10 kilometers from here.

My house is **very / really** far from here. It's 30 kilometers from here.

You can use *pretty* before adjectives and adverbs to soften the word. Compare:

My neighbors are quiet. I never hear them.

My neighbors are **pretty** quiet, but sometimes they talk loudly.

Do not use *pretty* when a sentence is negative.

Is your house far from here?

~~No, it isn't **pretty** far~~. No, it isn't far. *or* No, it isn't **very / really** far.

A Complete the sentences with *very*, *really*, or *pretty*. Sometimes, more than one answer is possible.

1. I don't know Jaime _____ well.

2. I'm _____ sure that guy over there is Leo, but I'm not certain.

3. There's a _____ old university in Fes el Bali. It opened in the year 859.

4. This apartment building is _____ new. It's about two years old.

5. You're driving _____ fast: almost 160 kilometers an hour. It's dangerous!

6. It's _____ easy to get from my house to school. The bus stops right in front of my house.

B 🔁 Compare your answers in **A** with a partner's. Are your answers the same? If not, explain your reasons.

UNIT 6 GOALS

LESSON A

Plans and Decisions with *be going* to and *will*			
I'm / You're / He's / She's / We're / They're	(not)	**going to** go to Harvard.	
Maybe	I / you / he / she / we / they	**will** **won't**	see a movie.

Contractions (*is / are*)
you're not = you aren't
she's not = she isn't
Contractions (*will*)
I'll / you'll / he'll / she'll / we'll / they'll

Use *be going to* to talk about future plans you have already made. (You thought about the plans beforehand.) *Good news! I'm going to attend Harvard in the fall.*

Use *will* for future events when you make a sudden decision at the time of speaking. (You didn't think about the plans beforehand.) *I don't have any plans tonight. Maybe I'll see a movie.*

A Complete the statements and questions with the correct form of *be going to*. Some items have more than one answer.

1. _____ (I / not) learn English in another country.

2. _____ (you) join a club on campus?

3. _____ (she) decide on a college soon.

4. _____ (they / not) pass the test.

5. _____ (she) take attendance?

6. _____ (we) live in a dorm room.

7. _____ (he / not) attend a private school.

8. _____ (they) finish their homework?

B Complete the sentences with the correct form of *be going to* or *will*.

1. I graduate from high school in June. Then I _____ attend college in the fall.

2. I'm bored and don't know what to do. Wait, I know... I _____ call my friend.

3. WAITER: What would you like today?

   CUSTOMER: Let's see... I _____ have the chicken and rice, please.

4. I bought my ticket last month. I _____ visit Paris from July 1 to July 14.

5. A: This box is too heavy!
   B: Wait! I _____ help you.

6. I _____ apply to three schools.

Predictions with *be going to* and *will*	
She's **going to** / **will** be very successful. Some students **aren't going to** / **won't** pass the exam.	You can use *be going to* and *will* to make predictions (guesses) about the future.
He'll <u>definitely</u> / <u>probably</u> study business in college. <u>Maybe</u> he'll study business in college. He <u>definitely</u> / <u>probably</u> **won't** study history.	You can use *definitely*, *probably*, or *maybe* to say how certain you are about something. Notice how they are used with *will* and *be going to*. *Definitely:* You are 100% certain of something.
She's <u>definitely</u> / <u>probably</u> **going to** attend college in the fall. <u>Maybe</u> she's **going to** get a job after graduation. She <u>definitely</u> / <u>probably</u> **isn't going to** go to college. / She's <u>definitely</u> / <u>probably</u> **not going to** go to college.	*Probably:* You are very certain of something. *Maybe:* You think something is possible.
A: **Is** she **going to** go to graduate school? B: <u>Maybe</u>. I'm not sure. A: **Will** she go to graduate school? B: <u>Probably not</u>. I think she wants to get a job.	You can ask a *Yes / No* prediction question with *be going to* or *will*. It's common to answer these questions with only *definitely*, *probably*, or *maybe*. To express the negative, add *not* after *definitely*, *probably*, or *maybe*.

A Answer each question with the words in parentheses and *be going to* or *will*. Some items may have more than one possible answer.

1. A: What are Mario's plans for next year?

   B: I'm not sure. _____ (he / go back to school / maybe).

2. A: Are Clara and Tony going to get married?

   B: Yeah, _____ (they / get married / definitely / someday).

3. A: Is Rob going to go to the school party tonight?

   B: _____ (not / go / probably / he). He's sick.

4. A: Jun applied to Seoul National University. It's hard to get accepted.

   B: I know, but _____ (get accepted / definitely / he). He's smart.

5. A: Where's the bus? It's late.

   B: _____ (probably / not / be / it) here for a while. Traffic is bad.

6. A: Is it going to rain tomorrow?

   B: Yeah, _____ (rain / it / probably) tomorrow, too.

B 🔁 Ask and answer the questions in **A** with a partner. In which dialogs can you use a short answer with *definitely*, *probably*, or *maybe*? Say them again with a partner.

LESSON A

Agreeing with Other People's Statements: *so, too, neither*, and *either*				
	Statements	**So / Neither**	**be / do**	**Subject**
Affirmative	*With be:* I'<u>m</u> going to Emi's party.	**So**	am	I.
			are	we.
	With other verbs: I <u>have</u> a costume for the party.	**So**	do	I.
				we.
Negative	*With be:* I'<u>m</u> <u>not</u> going to Emi's party.	**Neither**	am	I.
			are	we.
	With other verbs: I <u>don't have</u> a costume for the party.	**Neither**	do	I.
				we.

Responses like *So am I* or *Neither do we* can be used to agree with other people's statements.

Use *so* in your response when agreeing with an affirmative statement. Use *neither* when agreeing with a negative one.

These responses are most common in the first person singular: *So do <u>I</u>*. Other forms can also be used:
       Neither do <u>we</u>.

The tense in the response should match the tense used in the statements:
       A: *I <u>bought</u> my costume for the party.*   B: *So <u>did</u> I.*

You can also use this structure to combine two ideas:
       I like parties. Ali likes parties. → I like parties, and so does Ali.

In casual conversation, you can use *Me too* (with affirmative statements) or *Me neither* (with negative statements). They can both be used as responses to statements with *be* as well as other verbs:
       A: *I'm going to Emi's party. I have my costume ready.*   B: *Me too.*
       A: *I don't have my costume. I am not worried about it.*   B: *Me neither.*

	Statements	**Subject**	**be / do**	**too / either**
Affirmative	*With be:* I'<u>m</u> going to Emi's party.	I	am	**too.**
		We	are	
	With other verbs: I <u>have</u> a costume for the party.	I	do	**too.**
		We		
Negative	*With be:* I'<u>m</u> <u>not</u> going to Emi's party.	I	'm not	**either.**
		We	're not	
	With other verbs: I <u>don't have</u> a costume for the party.	I	don't	**either.**
		We		

Like the expressions with *so* and *neither*, you can use responses with *too* and *either* to agree with other people's statements.

Use *too* in your response when agreeing with an affirmative statement. Use *either* when agreeing with a negative one.

The tense in the response should match the tense used in the statements:
       A: *I <u>bought</u> my costume for the party.*   B: *I <u>did</u> too.*

You can also use this structure to combine two ideas:
       I like parties. Ali likes parties. → I like parties, and Ali does too.

A Agree with each statement in at least two ways.

1. I like to host parties.

_____

2. I'm never late to class.

_____

3. I don't speak Italian.

_____

4. I'm planning to study abroad next year.

_____

5. I did well on the exam.

_____

B Combine the sentences using the words in parentheses.

1. I'm having a good time. They're having a good time. (so)
   I'm having a good time, and so are they.

2. I throw a lot of parties. She throws a lot of parties. (so)

_____

3. I don't watch the Super Bowl. He doesn't watch the Super Bowl. (either)

_____

4. I'm inviting a lot of friends. They're inviting a lot of friends. (too)

_____

5. You don't celebrate the lunar New Year. We don't celebrate the lunar New Year. (neither)

_____

LESSON B

Time Clauses with *before, after, when*	
Time clause	**Main clause**
Before the festival starts,	Violetta speaks.
After the party ended,	we went home.
When you throw powder in the air,	you say "Holi Hai!"
Main clause	**Time clause**
Violetta speaks	**before** the festival starts.
We went home	**after** the party ended.
You say "Holi Hai!"	**when** you throw powder in the air.

A time clause shows the order of two or more events:
   In sentence 1: Violetta speaks. Then the festival starts.
   In sentence 2: The party ended. Then we went home.
   In sentence 3: The two events (You say "Holi Hai!" You throw powder in the air.) happen
   at almost the same time, or one happens immediately after the other.
When the time clause comes first, put a comma before the main clause.

A Combine the two sentences into one sentence using either *after*, *before*, or *when*. Use commas if necessary.

1. I brush my teeth. I eat breakfast.

   _____

2. My friends and I get together. We have a good time.

   _____

3. I get a present. I send a thank-you message.

   _____

4. Guests come to our house. We clean up.

   _____

5. A person takes the college entrance exam. He or she studies very hard.

   _____

6. A person turns 20 years old. He or she throws a big party.

   _____

B 🔁 Check your answers in **A** with a partner. Are the sentences in **A** true for you or your country? Why or why not?

> Before I eat breakfast,
> I brush my teeth.

> Really? I always brush
> my teeth after I eat!

UNIT **8** STORYTELLING

LESSON A

The Past Continuous Tense: Statements				
Subject	***was / were (not)***	**Verb + *ing***		
I He / She	was / wasn't	**studying**	English	at four o'clock. last summer. after lunchtime.
You We They	were / weren't			

Use the past continuous tense to talk about an action <u>in progress</u> in the past. The action can happen at a specific point in time or over a period of time.

We don't usually use the past continuous with stative verbs (*hear*, *need*, *know*, etc.).

Use the simple past, not the past continuous, to talk about a <u>completed</u> action:

   A: *I called you last night.*   B: *I <u>didn't hear</u> my phone. I <u>was watching</u> TV.*

You can use the past continuous with the simple past to show that one action was in progress when another action happened. Notice the use of *when*:

   I <u>was taking</u> a shower when the phone <u>rang</u>.

The Past Continuous Tense: Questions					
	Wh- word	**was / were**	**Subject**	**Verb +** *ing*	**Answers**
Yes / No questions		Were	you they	**reading** a story?	Yes, I was. / No, I wasn't. Yes, they were. / No, they weren't.
		Was	she		Yes, she was. / No, she wasn't.
Wh- questions	What	were	you they	**reading?**	(I was reading) (They were reading) a story.
		was	he		(He was reading) a story.

A Read the story. Find the eight grammar errors and correct them.

Last summer, I'm eating dinner in a restaurant with two friends. We were talking and laughing when I was noticing a woman coming in. It was very hot outside, but the woman was wearing a heavy winter coat. The restaurant was nearly empty, but she was sitting next to our table anyway. The woman was looking at me for a second and gave me a friendly smile. After that, I forgot about her.

Later on, we was paying our bill and getting ready to go home when one of my friends was realizing that his wallet was missing from his back pocket. We were calling the police, and they came right away. Unfortunately, I wasn't seeing anything, so I couldn't help very much. As it turned out, the police knew the woman and were looking for her. They never found her, and my friend never got his money back.

B Complete the sentences with the past continuous or simple past form of the verb.

1. They (have) _____ a good time when the woman (come) _____ in.

2. The woman (give) _____ a friendly smile when she (sit) _____ down.

3. They (notice) _____ the wallet was missing when they (pay) _____ the bill.

4. They (call) _____ the police when they (notice) _____ the theft.

5. They told the police they (see / not) _____ anything when the woman (take) _____ the wallet.

LESSON B

Adverbs of Manner	
Cinderella smiled **shyly** at the prince.	**Adverbs of manner** describe how something is done. Many end in *-ly*, and they often come after a verb.
He opened the door **quietly**. She answered the question **correctly**. *Not: He opened quietly the door.* *She answered correctly the question.*	When there is an object (a noun or pronoun) after the verb, the adverb usually comes at the end of the sentence.
She was different from other children. You seem unhappy.	Remember: Adjectives, not adverbs, come after stative verbs (words like *be*, *have*, *hear*, *need*, *know*, *seem*).
She drives too **fast**. He studied **hard** for the exam. They didn't do **well** in school.	Some common adverbs of manner don't end in *-ly*. Some examples are: *fast*, *hard*, and *well*.

A   Rewrite each sentence using the adverb form of the word in parentheses. Use a different verb if necessary.

1. He is fluent in three languages. (fluent)

    He speaks three languages fluently.

2. In the famous story, the hare is a fast runner, and the tortoise is a slow walker. (quick, slow)

    _____

3. In the movie *Star Wars*, Luke Skywalker is a brave fighter. (brave)

    _____

4. When she left the party, Cinderella lost a shoe. (accident)

    _____

5. In the story, the man disappears in a mysterious way. (mysterious)

    _____

6. The girl is only six, but she is a very good singer. (good)

    _____

B   In five minutes, how many sentences can you make with the words below? Time yourself. You can use present or past forms of the verbs. Compare your answers with a partner's.

boy	girl	dragon	song
fight	run	sing	struggle with
beautifully	bravely	fast / quickly	slowly

The boy and girl fought the dragon bravely.

LESSON A

The Present Perfect Tense: Statements				
Subect	*have / has (not)*	**Past participle**		
I / You	**have** haven't	**worked**	there	for six months.
He / She	**has** hasn't			
We / You / They	**have** haven't			

<table>
<tr><td colspan="2">Contractions</td></tr>
<tr><td colspan="2">I have = I've</td></tr>
<tr><td colspan="2">she has = she's</td></tr>
<tr><td colspan="2">we have = we've</td></tr>
<tr><td colspan="2">have not = haven't</td></tr>
<tr><td colspan="2">has not = hasn't</td></tr>
</table>

Use the present perfect to talk about an action that started in the past and continues up to now. Notice the difference:

simple past: *I worked there for six months, and then I quit.* (action finished)

present perfect: *I've worked there for six months. I love my job!* (action continuing)

Base, Simple Past, and Past Participle Forms								
Regular verbs			**Irregular verbs**					
Base	**Simple past**	**Past participle**	**Base**	**Simple past**	**Past participle**	**Base**	**Simple past**	**Past participle**
call	called	called	be	was/were	been	leave	left	left
change	changed	changed	become	became	become	make	made	made
live	lived	lived	begin	began	begun	put	put	put
look	looked	looked	come	came	come	read	read	read
move	moved	moved	do	did	done	say	said	said
study	studied	studied	drink	drank	drunk	see	saw	seen
talk	talked	talked	find	found	found	sleep	slept	slept
try	tried	tried	get	got	gotten	speak	spoke	spoken
use	used	used	give	gave	given	take	took	taken
want	wanted	wanted	go	went	gone	tell	told	told
work	worked	worked	have	had	had	think	thought	thought
			know	knew	known	write	wrote	written

Use the past participle after *have / has* to form the present perfect.

Verbs that are regular in the simple past take the same *ed* ending for the past participle: *talk / talked / talked*.

Verbs that are irregular in the simple past have irregular past participle forms: *speak / spoke / spoken*.

The Present Perfect Tense: *Wh-* Questions					
Wh- word	*have / has*	**Subject**	**Past participle**		**Answers**
How long	**have**	you	**worked**	there?	(I**'ve worked** there) for two years.
	has	she			(She**'s worked** there) since 2012.

Use *for* + a length of time (*for two years, for a long time, for the entire summer, for my whole life*).

Use *since* + a point in time (*since 2014, since last September, since Friday, since I was a child*).

A On a piece of paper, make as many sentences in the present perfect as you can using the words below.

They He We	has have	been worked	a flight attendant friends at that company	for since	elementary school. a long time.

B Complete the profiles. Use the present perfect form of the verbs in parentheses and *for* or *since*.

"I (1. live) _____ in the United States (2.) _____
August. I (3. study) _____ English (4.) _____
I was in high school. I'm studying for an exam right now.
I (5. not / sleep) _____ well (6.) _____
two days. I (7. drink) _____ three cups of coffee
(8.) _____ 9:00."

"He (1. be) _____ in college (2.) _____ three
years. He (3. not / come) _____ home (4.) _____ a
year. I miss him. He (5. live) _____ overseas
(6.) _____ 2012. We (7. not / talk) _____ on the
phone (8.) _____ a month."

LESSON B

Verb + Infinitive	
I **like** to sing. I **want** to be a singer. She **needed** to move to London for work. I've **tried** to get a job for a month, but it's not easy.	Certain **verbs** can be followed by an <u>infinitive</u> (*to* + verb). See below for a list. Note: The **main verb** can be in different tenses.

These verbs can be followed by an infinitive:

agree	attempt	decide	forget	hope	like	need	prepare	try
arrange	choose	expect	hate	learn	love	plan	start	want

A Read each sentence. Then do the following:

- Underline the main verb.

- Which verbs are followed by an infinitive? Circle the infinitive forms. Not all the sentences have one.

1. They <u>agree</u> (to do) the job.

2. I chose to go to a large university.

3. I need a snack before I go to bed.

4. I like to buy presents for my friends.

5. I forgot the key to this door.

6. He hopes to meet her parents.

7. I expect him at ten minutes to three.

8. Can you prepare to give the report?

B Complete the sentences below with the infinitive form of the verbs in the box.

go	help	open	attend	work	become	graduate	perform	sing	work

SANJAY: I've always liked (1.) _to speak_ foreign languages. I decided (2.) _____ as an interpreter. I work at the United Nations.

TERESA: I chose (3.) _____ to medical school because I wanted (4.) _____ people. I'm planning (5.) _____ a clinic in my hometown.

DAN: My sister is learning (6.) _____. She wants (7.) _____ in an opera someday.

CAMILLE: I want (8.) _____ a flight attendant. I need (9.) _____ a six-week training course. I expect (10.) _____ in August and to start (11.) _____ in September.

UNIT **10** TELEPHONING

LESSON A

Asking for Permission							Responses
❶ Would	it be OK						Certainly. / Of course. / Sure, no problem. (I'm) sorry, but…
❷ Would	you mind	if	I	used	your phone?		No, not at all. / No, go ahead. (I'm) sorry, but…
❸ Do	you mind	if	I	use	your phone?		No, not at all. / No, go ahead. (I'm) sorry, but…
❹ May / Could / Can			I	use	your phone?		Certainly. / Of course. / Sure, no problem. (I'm) sorry, but…

❶ & ❷ The use of the past tense verb (e.g., *used*) makes requests with *Would* sound slightly more polite or formal.

❷ & ❸ To agree to a request made with *Would you mind / Do you mind*, answer with *no* (e.g., *No, I don't mind. You can use my phone.*)

❹ *May I* and *Could I* are slightly more formal than *Can I.*

A Unscramble the words to make questions.

1. you / I / messages / would / my / if / text / mind / checked

   _____

2. him / a / leave / could / message / I

   _____

3. OK / turned / it / phone / be / on / would / I / my / if

   _____

4. make / can / a / call / home / phone / I / quick

   _____

B 🔁 Complete the dialogs. Then practice them with a partner.

1. A: _____ _____ mind if I opened the window?

   B: _____, not _____ _____. It's really hot in here.

2. A: May _____ _____ here?

   B: _____ _____, but my friend is sitting there.

3. A: _____ _____ mind if I turn up the volume a bit? It's hard to hear.

   B: _____, _____ ahead.

4. A: _____ _____ _____ OK if I didn't turn in my homework today?

   B: _____, no _____. Just turn it in tomorrow.

C On a separate piece of paper, write the opposite responses to each question in **B**.

LESSON B

Verb + Infinitive vs. Verb + Gerund	
I **need** <u>to buy</u> a new phone.	Certain verbs can be followed by an <u>infinitive</u> (*to* + verb).
I **avoid** <u>talking</u> on the phone when I'm driving.	Other verbs can be followed by a <u>gerund</u> (verb + *-ing*).
I **tried** <u>to call</u> / <u>calling</u> you earlier.	Some verbs can be followed by an infinitive or a gerund.

Verbs followed by an infinitive		Verbs followed by a gerund		Verbs followed by an infinitive or a gerund	
agree	need	appreciate	finish	begin	love
choose	plan	avoid	imagine	can't stand	prefer
decide	seem	dislike	keep	hate	start
hope	want	enjoy	(not) mind	like	try
learn	would like	feel like	suggest		

A Underline the gerund or the infinitive in each sentence. Then check (✓) the correct sentences. Change the incorrect sentences.

1. ☐ I learned to speak Spanish in high school.

2. ☐ I avoid to call people on the phone.

3. ☐ I began to raise my voice.

4. ☐ I enjoy to play games on my phone.

5. ☐ I agreed turning down the music on my phone.

6. ☐ I prefer to respond to texts quickly.

7. ☐ I finished to do my homework and then I called a friend.

8. ☐ I tried texting you twice but you didn't reply.

B Complete each question with the infinitive or gerund form of the word in parentheses. Sometimes both forms are possible.

1. What do you need (do) _____to do_____ this weekend?

2. Who's someone you'd like (meet) _____?

3. What's something you can't stand (do) _____?

4. When did you start (learn) _____ English?

5. What TV shows do you enjoy (watch) _____?

C Now answer the questions in **B**. Use complete sentences.

Example: _I love hanging out with my friends._ _____

1. _____

2. _____

3. _____

4. _____

5. _____

UNIT **11** TECHNOLOGY

LESSON A

Used to			
Subject	**use(d) to**	**Verb**	
I	**used to**	wear	glasses.
We	didn't **use to**	own	a computer.

Use *used to* for habits and actions that happened during a period of time in the past but are no longer happening now: *I used to wear glasses, but now I wear contacts.*

Use a time expression like *now* or *today* to make a contrast between the present and the past:
We didn't use to own a computer, but now we have three of them at home.

Expressions like *nowadays* and *these days* can be used for people or events "in general":
People used to use their phones only for making calls. These days, they use them to do lots of things.

Notice the spelling of *use to* in negative statements.

Did	**Subject**	*use to*	**Verb**		**Responses**
Did	you	use to	wear	glasses?	Yes, I did. / No, I didn't.
	she		own	a computer?	Yes, she did. / No, she didn't.

Notice the spelling of *use to* in questions.

A Complete the sentences about *used to*.

1. Use *used to* to talk about the   a. present.   b. past.

2. *Used to* is followed by   a. the base form of a verb.   b. a gerund (*ing* form).

3. Use *use to* in negative statements and   a. responses.   b. questions.

B Write sentences to compare life today with life 100 years ago. Use the time expressions given. Follow the model.

1. People had bigger families. (nowadays)

People used to have bigger families. Nowadays families are smaller.

2. Not many people owned a television. (today)

3. Not many women worked outside of the home. (now)

4. Telephones weren't portable. (these days)

5. Technology wasn't affordable. (now)

6. People read books instead of watching TV. (today)

LESSON B

Comparisons with *as... as*	

Phone A is 12 cm. Phone B is 12 cm.
   Phone A is **as** <u>big</u> **as** phone B.
 	
Phone A costs $100. Phone B costs $100.
   Phone A costs **as** <u>much</u> **as** phone B.
	Use *as* + adjective / adverb + *as* to show that two things are equal.

Camera A isn't **as** <u>affordable</u> **as** Camera B. Maria didn't do **as** <u>well</u> **as** Carlos on the test.	You can use *not as... as* to show that things are not equal.
My phone works **as** well **as** <u>your phone</u>. = My phone works **as** well **as** <u>yours</u>. I like this phone **as** much **as** that <u>phone</u>. = I like this phone **as** much **as** that <u>one</u>. She studies **as** hard **as** <u>he studies</u>. (not common) She studies **as** hard **as** <u>he does</u>. (common) She studies **as** hard **as** <u>him</u>.	Sometimes after *as... as*, you can end a sentence with a pronoun. In spoken and written English, it's common not to repeat the main verb after *as... as*, but to say things as shown in the example.

A Unscramble the sentences.

1. speaks / She / as / you / English / do / well / as

   _____

2. us / don't / as / have / many / You / classes / as

   _____

3. computer / heavy / as / This / isn't / as / one / that

   _____

4. My / durable / as / tablet / as / isn't / yours

   _____

5. jacket / as / That / is / this / one / as / fashionable

   _____

B Compare the two vacuum cleaners in the chart by completing the sentences with *(not) as… as*. There may be more than one possible correct answer.

	The Vacuum Star	The Vacuum Pro
weight	6 kilos	6 kilos
price	$450	$150
durability	lasts 5–10 years	lasts 4–5 years
popularity	☆☆☆	☆☆☆☆☆
convenience	Robotic; cleans everywhere by itself	Robotic; cleans everywhere by itself

1. weight

   The Vacuum Star ___weighs as much as___ the Vacuum Pro. / The Vacuum Star ___is as heavy as___ the Vacuum Pro.

2. price

   The Vacuum Pro _____ the Vacuum Star.

3. durability

   The Vacuum Pro _____ the Vacuum Star.

4. popularity

   The Vacuum Star _____ the Vacuum Pro.

5. convenience

   The Vacuum Star _____ the Vacuum Pro.

UNIT 12 TRAVEL

LESSON A

Modal Verbs of Necessity		
	Present forms	**Past forms**
Affirmative	You **must** show your ID to get on the plane. I **have to** buy a backpack for my trip. We**'ve got to** get some cash.	I **had to** wait at the airport for an hour.
Negative	I **don't have to** check any luggage.	I **didn't have to** wait long.

Use *must*, *have to*, and *have got to* + the base form of a verb to say that something is necessary.

In spoken and written English, *have to* is used most commonly.

Must is often used to talk about rules or laws. *Must* is stronger than *have (got) to*.

Only *have to* can be used in the negative or to talk about things that were necessary in the past.

A Correct the error in each sentence.

1. She doesn't has to pack her suitcase. _____

2. They must leave yesterday. _____

3. I haven't to water the plants. _____

4. All passengers must to board the flight now. _____

5. We didn't had to pay in cash. _____

6. You don't have got to confirm your flight. _____

7. He got to give his house keys to a friend. _____

LESSON B

Present Perfect (Indefinite Time) vs. Simple Past		
Statements	I**'ve been** to Korea.	He**'s booked** his flight.
Questions and answers	**Have** you (ever) **been** to Brazil? Yes, I have. I **was** there last year.* No, I haven't. No, I've never been there.	**Have** you **packed** yet? Yes, I've already packed. Yes, I've packed already. No, I haven't packed yet.

Use the present perfect to talk about past actions when the time they happened is unknown or unimportant.

Note: When you answer a present perfect question with a specific time expression, use the simple past.

  Have you ever visited Brazil?

  Yes, I visited in 2015.   Yes, I was there two years ago.

Adverbs used with the present perfect

Ever means "at any time in the past up to now." It is optional.

Never means "at no time in the past."

Use *yet* or *already* to talk about whether an action has been completed or not.

Use *yet* in questions and negative statements. Use *already* in affirmative statements.

A Read each dialog and the statement below it. Write *T* for *true*, *F* for *false*, or *N* for *not enough information*.

1. Man: Do you want a sandwich?

   Woman: I've already eaten, thanks.

   • The woman is hungry. _____

2. Man: Have you been to the check-in counter yet?

   Woman: Not yet.

   • The woman isn't ready to get on the plane. _____

3. Man: Should I call a cab for you?

   Woman: No, It's OK. I've already called one.

   • A cab is coming soon. _____

4. Woman: What does Maria want?

   Man: I don't know, but she's called three times.

   • Maria called an hour ago. _____

5. Man: Are you excited about your trip to London?

   Woman: I am. I've never been there.

   • This is the woman's first visit to London. _____

6. Woman: Where are the suitcases?

   Man: I've already put them in the car.

   • The man still has to put the suitcases in the car. _____

B Unscramble the questions.

1. ever / traveled / you / somewhere alone / have

   _____

2. a passport / have / you / yet / gotten

   _____

3. this year / already / you / a trip / taken / have

   _____

4. you / made any plans / have / for summer vacation / yet

   _____

5. lost / an airline / your luggage / ever / has

   _____

C Answer the questions in **B** about yourself. Use short answers. If the things are true, say when they happened.

1. _____

2. _____

3. _____

4. _____

5. _____